The QBasic Reference Book

Ian Sinclair

GW00641776

Bruce Smith Books

QBasic Reference Book

© Ian Sinclair 1993.

ISBN: 1-873308-22-1   First Edition: September 1993.

Editors: Mark Webb and Peter Fitzpatrick
Typesetting: Bruce Smith Books Ltd.
Cover design: Jude at *Wire Design Studio*
Internal design: Steve Prickett/*image*MAKERS.

Bruce Smith Books is an imprint of Bruce Smith Books Limited.

Published by
Bruce Smith Books Limited. PO Box 382, St. Albans, Herts, AL2 3JD.
Telephone: (0923) 894355, Fax: (0923) 894366

Registered in England No. 2695164.
Registered Office: 51 Quarry Street, Guildford, Surrey, GU1 3UA.

Printed and bound in the UK by Bell & Bain.

The Author

With over 150 books on computer-related subjects under his belt since 1972, Ian Sinclair brings a wealth of both writing and technical experience to his work. Born in 1932 and educated at St Andrews university, he worked in radar display systems before moving into lecturing and then writing full-time.

Ian lives in the heart of glorious Suffolk and writes full-time, accompanied by the sounds of Classic FM.

QBASIC Book

Perfect PC series

This brand new book is part of the Perfect PC series from Bruce Smith Books, Britain's fastest growing publisher of computer books. We've gained a reputation for technical excellence, coupled with an easy to read informal style which makes reading a pleasure.

All our books are by UK authors writing about UK software versions.

As a specialist publisher, Bruce Smith Books seeks to provide a full and efficient service to its readers. Call the editors or write to the author, we are happy to hear from you.

Contents

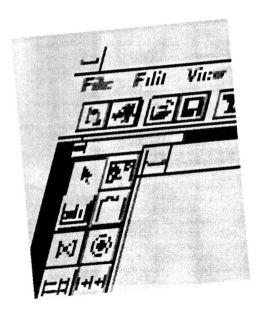

Preface

QBASIC, by being packaged along with MS-DOS 5.0 and subsequent issues of MS-DOS, has become the most widely available version of BASIC since the venerable GW-BASIC. Unlike its predecessor, QBASIC is a modern version that requires no line numbering, makes use of a full-screen editor, and which includes many forms of commands that are alien to older types of BASIC, such as SELECT...CASE, DO...UNTIL, and also such innovations to BASIC as user-defined data types (records).

Because of the need to retain some compatibility with older versions of BASIC, QBASIC has retained most of the commands of GW-BASIC, though some in enhanced form, as well as adding its own. This has made the set of reserved words very large and, though the built-in HELP pages are useful, it is difficult to work from them while designing a program. In addition, HELP pages are always restricted in the amount of help that can be usefully provided on screen.

This book is designed as a companion to *The QBASIC Beginners Book* in order to provide a list of keywords along with detailed explanation, examples, hints and warnings about the use of the various functions, statements and operators of QBASIC. *The QBASIC Beginners Book* is a primer of QBASIC; this book is a companion for the keen programmer who needs to be able quickly to look up the syntax of a reserved word or to check that a statement in an existing program can be used in a QBASIC program.

Each keyword is dealt with in strict alphabetical order, following a uniform pattern of description. Invariably, this means that some keywords will be dealt with very briefly and others will require several pages. The aim is to ensure that the information is easy to reach and to understand.

Where a keyword is that of a function, the returned value is shown as string of number (showing whether the number in integer, long-integer, represents an operator, the type of operator (arithmetic, logic) is stated and the type of result of the action.

In some cases, a complete statement can consist of several keywords that are always associated, such as OPEN...FOR...AS. Rather than use cross-references, all the keywords have been dealt with. This causes some duplication of information, but it makes the book easier to use, with no need to search for cross references other than to check the effects of associated statements. Data such as colour numbers and keycodes is also printed under more than one reference for convenience.

The examples are as short as they can be made without losing the context for each keyword. As far as possible, the spacing that is used is that required by QBASIC, but spaces have been compressed in some examples for easier printing. This is of no importance, because the QBASIC editor will correct the spacing each time you press the Enter (Return) key.

I am grateful in compilation of this book to Microsoft UK Ltd for information on QBASIC, to Bruce Smith Books Ltd for encouragement and to Henry Kelly and Petroc Trelawny of Classic FM for providing amicable background music.

Ian Sinclair.

ABS

Type:	Function returning positive number
Typical syntax:	numvariable = ABS(number)
Action:	Strips off any negative sign from a number, number variable or expression that returns a number. This returns a number that has size but not sign, an absolute value.
Options:	None
Argument(s):	Any number, number-variable or expression that will provide a number, enclosed in brackets.
Restrictions:	Using a string as an argument will cause a *Type Mismatch* error, number 13 (see Appendix E).

Example:

```
A% = 50             'assign
B% = 25             'variables
PRINT (A% - B%)     'print difference
PRINT ABS(B% - A%)  'this gives same answer of 25
```

Associated with: SGN

Points to note:

Use when the presence of a sign may be misleading, such as in a distance. The use of ABS should be considered in any statement in which one number variable is subtracted from another.

ABSOLUTE

Type: Statement

Typical syntax: CALL ABSOLUTE(data,offset)

Action: CALL ABSOLUTE will run the machine-code routine which starts at the provided address. This routine will normally end with a return to the calling program.

Options: The data argument can be omitted unless variable values need to be passed from the QBASIC program to the machine-code routine. Such arguments are in the form of pointer address numbers in the data segment.

Argument(s): Data, as above, and an offset for the starting address of a machine-code routine in the code segment, all enclosed in brackets.

Restrictions: Can be used only following CALL. Using an incorrect pointer address will usually cause the machine to hang up, requiring a reboot.

Example:

```
CALL ABSOLUTE (12116, 7114)
REM will start a machine-code routine located
REM at address 7114 (denary) in the code segment,
REM passing the address of an integer variable starting
REM at address 12116 in the current data segment.
```

Associated with: CALL, DEF SEG, VARPTR, VARSEG

Points to note:

This form of CALL should be used only by an experienced machine-code programmer. The DEF SEG statement needs to be used to ensure that the correct segment is in use before the CALL ABSOLUTE is made. See Appendix C for details of the segmented addressing system of the PC type of machines.

ACCESS

Type:	Statement
Typical syntax:	OPEN name$ FOR output ACCESS write AS filenumber
Action:	Provides network access to files for reading, writing or both, depending on the argument used.
Options:	None
Argument(s):	READ, WRITE, READ WRITE
Restrictions:	Must be used along with OPEN statement. Applies only to *networked* files for which it specifies the form of access permitted.

Example:

```
OPEN "Myfile" FOR RANDOM ACCESS READWRITE AS #1
OPEN "Newfile" FOR INPUT ACCESS READ AS #2
OPEN "Oldfile" FOR OUTPUT ACCESS WRITE AS #3
```

Associated with: AS, FOR, LOCK, OPEN, UNLOCK

Points to note:

Should not be used unless the network action and requirements are thoroughly understood. ACCESS needs to be used only if you are writing a database application for use on a networked system.

AND

Type:	Operator returning Boolean TRUE or FALSE
Typical syntax:	Result = Expression1 AND Expression2
Action:	Result of AND is TRUE (-1) or FALSE (0) only. A TRUE result is returned only if both expressions are TRUE. As a table, this is:

Expression1	Expression 2	Result
FALSE	FALSE	FALSE
FALSE	TRUE	FALSE
TRUE	FALSE	FALSE
TRUE	TRUE	TRUE

Options:	None
Argument(s):	Two variables or expressions placed one before and one after AND. Any expression is converted into an integer or long integer before the comparison is made.
Restrictions:	Each expression must be capable of being resolved as TRUE or FALSE. The precedence of the AND operator is low, following arithmetic and relational operations. AND should not be used with numbers, see notes.

Examples:

(a)
```
IF (Age% > 65) AND (NOT Mortgage) THEN  'AND test
    call discuss                   'do if TRUE
END IF
REM The quantity Mortgage must be either 0 or -1
REM - a Boolean quantity.
```

(b)
```
IF B$ <> "END" AND count% <= 100 THEN     ' AND test
    EXIT DO                               ' leave loop
END IF
```

Associated with: EQV, IMP, NOT, OR, XOR

Points to note:

Using expressions that provide values other than 0 for false and -1 for true will produce unexpected results. For example, 7 AND 11 gives the result 5 because the AND action on each bit of the binary numbers is:

(7)	0111
(11)	1101
0101	which is 5.

ANY

Type:	Statement
Typical syntax:	DECLARE subname (varname AS ANY)
	DECLARE FUNCTION newname (varname AS ANY)
Action:	Allows the named variable, which will be passed to a subroutine or a defined function, to be of any type. The permitted types are INTEGER, LONG, SHORT, DOUBLE, STRING or a user-defined type (see TYPE).
Options:	None
Argument(s):	None
Restrictions:	Can be used only following AS in a declaration for a subroutine or defined function, to declare the type of a parameter. Note the use of brackets around the declaration.

Example:

```
DECLARE SUB testit (namit AS ANY)  'can use any parameter
.........................          'other statements
CALL testit ("sort")               'call, passing string
CALL testit (A%)                   'call passing integer
```

Associated with: CALL, FUNCTION, SUB

Points to note:

When a specified type such as INTEGER, DOUBLE, LONG, SINGLE or STRING, is used, the data that is passed to a SUB or FUNCTION is checked to ensure that it is of the correct type. When ANY is used, this checking is suspended. If the SUB or FUNCTION cannot deal correctly with any possible data type an error will occur inside the procedure or function.

APPEND

Type:	Statement
Typical syntax:	OPEN filename FOR APPEND AS number
Action:	Allows new data to be appended to an existing sequential file rather than replacing the existing data, as is done when OUTPUT is used in place of APPEND.
Options:	None
Argument(s):	None
Restrictions:	Used only in an OPEN statement following FOR. APPEND is applicable to sequential files only.

Example:

```
OPEN "Cats" FOR APPEND AS #5
PRINT #5, A$
REM will add the data in A$ to the existing data in
REM the CATS file.
```

Associated with: BINARY, INPUT, NAME, OPEN, OUTPUT, PRINT, WRITE

Points to note:

APPEND can be used even if a file has not been created. Its action is then the same as that of OPEN, creating the file and writing the data. It is therefore better to use APPEND for opening a serial file for writing unless you specifically want any file of the same name to be deleted. Use NAME to rename an old file if OPEN is used with the same name – this allows a new file to be opened with the old file retained as a BAK file.

AS

Type:	Statement
Typical syntax:	DIM name AS type
	name AS type
	OPEN filename FOR filetype AS number
	FIELD number AS variable
	NAME oldfilename AS newfilename
Action:	Nominates a name or number to be used with the preceding statement.
Options:	None
Argument(s):	Depend on context:
	Variable type in declarations
	Element in TYPE statement
	File number in OPEN statement
	Field name in FIELD statement
	File name in NAME statement
Restrictions:	Can be used only in association with DIM, FIELD, NAME, OPEN, TYPE statements.

Examples:

```
DECLARE varnam AS INTEGER      'declares type for variable name
TYPE datacard
   Surname AS STRING * 20      'declares fixed-length strings
   Forename AS STRING * 12     'in the variable type
END TYPE
OPEN "myfile" FOR INPUT AS #1  'establishes file reference number
FIELD #2, 25 AS person$        'establishes field size
NAME "oldfile" AS "newfile"    'establishes new name for file
```

Associated with: COMMON, DECLARE, DEF FN, DIM, REDIM, FIELD, FUNCTION, NAME, OPEN, SHARED, STATIC, SUB, TYPE

Points to note:

Because of the large variety of statements in which AS can be used it is easy to provide the wrong form of argument.

ASC

Type:	Function returning an integer
Typical syntax:	PRINT ASC(string)
	intvariable = ASC(string)
Action:	Returns the ASCII code (0 to 255) for a character, the first character of a string variable if the variable contains more than one character.
Options:	None
Argument(s):	A string of one or more characters. This can be a literal such as 'A' or a string variable, enclosed in brackets.
Restrictions:	Only the first character of a string will be used. If the string argument is a null-string, an *Illegal function call* error, Error 5, is produced when the program runs.

Examples:

(a)
```
A% = ASC(X$)              'A% holds ASCII character
```

(b)
```
FOR N% = 1 TO LEN(name$)            'print ASCII codes for
    PRINT ASC(MID$(name$, N%, 1)); 'all the characters
NEXT                                'in a name
```

Associated with: CHR$

Points to note:

If used with a string that has been obtained from a number by using STR$, the first character is usually a blank, ASCII 32. Blanks can be removed by using the LTRIM$ function. If a string might be null, test before using ASC with a test such as:

```
IF A$ = "" THEN
  PRINT "Null string"
  CALL noconvert        'routine for null string
  ELSE CALL convert     'routine for character present
END IF
```

ATN

Type:	Function returning double-precision number
Typical syntax:	X = ATN(number)
Action:	Returns the angle, in units of radians, whose tangent is the argument of the ATN function.
Options:	None
Argument(s):	A number which must be a possible trigonometrical tangent. Positive or negative numbers can be used, enclosed in brackets.
Restrictions:	The argument should not be very large or very small. Values smaller than 0.001 or larger than 500 provide results of low accuracy.

Example:

```
leng1 = 22.64                       'assign
leng2 = 24.66                       'assign
PRINT "Angle is "; ATN(leng1 / leng2)   'find angle between
                                    ' in radians
```

Associated with: COS, SIN, TAN

Points to note:

The returned angle is in units of radians – to convert to degrees multiply by 180 and divide by PI. A negative value of argument gives a negative angle. The radian-degree conversion can be carried out by using a defined function.

BASE

Type:	Statement
Typical syntax:	OPTION BASE base%
Action:	Sets the lower number to be used for array subscripts. The default is 0, so that the first member of an array A$() is A$(0). This can be changed, to A$(1), by using OPTION BASE.
Options:	None
Argument(s):	0 or 1 only. If OPTION BASE is not used, all arrays will use 0 for their lowest subscript.
Restrictions:	Used only following OPTION. Any attempt to use numbers other than 0 or 1 will be rejected by the editor.

Example:

```
OPTION BASE 1 'all arrays have lowest member 1
OPTION BASE 0 'all arrays have lowest member 0
```

Associated with: DIM, REDIM, LBOUND, UBOUND

Points to note:

Using OPTION BASE affects all arrays. The DIM...TO form is a better way of setting both lower and upper bounds for individual arrays, and provides a greater range – it is not limited to 0 or 1, so that arrays can be created which do not waste space with unnecessary subscript numbers.

BEEP

Type: Statement

Typical syntax: BEEP

Action: A BEEP statement produces a note of 800 Hz from the loudspeaker for 0.25 seconds. Musically, this is approximately a G in the octave above that of Middle C.

Options: None

Argument(s): None

Restrictions: None

Example:

```
PRINT "Pay attention"     'screen message
BEEP                      'sound
SLEEP 1                   'pause for thought
```

Associated with: PLAY, SOUND

Points to note:

As a way of producing a note, BEEP is very restricted in comparison to PLAY and SOUND. The BEEP action is equivalent to using PRINT CHR$(7), the ASCII Bell character. Computing actions are not suspended while the BEEP note is being sounded; this is a background action.

BINARY

Type:	Statement
Typical syntax:	OPEN name FOR BINARY AS number
Action:	Allows a file to be opened as a binary (character) file using PUT and GET to place and to read individual characters (single bytes).
Options:	None
Argument(s):	None
Restrictions:	Must follow OPEN

Example:

```
OPEN "Binfile" FOR BINARY AS #1      'open existing binary file
FOR J% = 0 TO 99                      'loop count
   GET #1, 1000 + J%, X$              'read character, move on
   A$ = A$ + X$                       'add into A$
NEXT                                  'get next until end
REM will open a file and read 100 characters into a variable A$
REM starting at position 1000 in the file.
REM each GET moves the start position on by one place.
```

Associated with: GET, LOF, OPEN, PUT, SEEK

Points to note:
Some older forms of BASIC use GET without the option to specify the file position. For these older versions, the position in the file must be correctly specified initially using SEEK. If this is not done a newly opened file will be read or written at the start; a file which has been used previously will be used starting at the position where the previous action left off. The QBASIC enhancement of GET allows older programs to be rewritten in a more compact form.

BLOAD

Type: Statement

Typical syntax: BLOAD filename, offsetnumber

Action: Loads the content of a disk file into the area of memory from which it was saved using BSAVE, or to a new set of addresses.

Options: An offset number (0 to 65535) for a starting address can be specified, in which case the loading starts at this address in the segment.

Argument(s): The filename must be that of a previously saved file created by BSAVE. If no offset is used, the data will be loaded back into the part of the memory it was saved from. It is unusual to need to alter the address.

Restrictions: Applies only to data contained as a consecutive set of bytes in memory. Use on CGA screens only because of problems with EGA and VGA screens.

Example:

```
BLOAD "memdump"
```

Associated with: BSAVE, DEF SEG, VARPTR, VARPTR$

Points to note:

You need to know the correct segment to use and what memory offset addresses will be needed, also the number of bytes to save. If an address is supplied, it must be a valid address – an incorrect address could result in wiping out MS-DOS or QBASIC itself. Some knowledge of machine code helps considerably. See also BSAVE comments.

BSAVE

Type:	Statement
Typical syntax:	BSAVE filename, address, length
Action:	Copies a specified number of bytes from the part of the memory determined by the current segment setting and the address offset number into a named file.
Options:	None
Argument(s):	The filename follows normal MS-DOS restrictions. The address (0 to 65535) specifies a starting position in the segment being used, the length number is the number of bytes to copy (0 to 65535).
Restrictions:	Avoid use with EGA and VGA screens.

Example:

```
DEF SEG = &HB000        `set mono screen memory
BSAVE "PIX", 0, 4000 `save monochrome screen
```

Associated with: BLOAD, DEF SEG, VARPTR, VARPTR$

Points to note:

This statement was used in versions of BASIC designed when all screen types were monochrome or CGA. It has little or no place with modern VGA screens. To save and load graphics, use PUT and GET and then save/load the resulting arrays.

The addresses used for text mode by the various VGA screen modes are listed below, along with the other screen systems that can make use of some of the modes. The numbers shown as segment numbers are as used for DEF SEG, in hex, and the address number to use with each will be 0.

Mode	DEF SEG	Bytes/page	Also used by
0,1	&HB800	2000	CGA, EGA, MCGA
2,3	&HB800	4000	CGA, EGA, MCGA
4,5	&HB800	16000	CGA, EGA, MCGA
6	&HB800	16000	CGA, EGA, MCGA
7	&HB000	4000	EGA

CALL

Type: Statement

Typical syntax: CALL subname (arguments)

Action: Transfers control to a SUB procedure, passing parameters as required to the procedure and using the same variable names to receive changed parameters if the procedure makes any changes.

Options: Can be used with or without arguments. An argument can be used in a way that prevents its value being changed, see below.

Argument(s): Any parameters to be passed in to or out from the procedure. An array argument must use the array name followed by empty brackets, such as arnam().

Restrictions: If the CALL keyword is omitted, there must normally be no brackets around the arguments. If CALL is omitted, brackets around a variable parameter mean that the value of that variable must *not* be changed by the procedure.

Example:

```
CALL printname (A$,B$,C(5))      'call SUB
.....................            'other statements
SUB getname (sur$,fore$,num(n%)) 'SUB header
PRINT sur$; ","; fore$           ' action
PRINT "Reference "; num(n%)      ' action
END SUB                          'end
```

Associated with: CALL ABSOLUTE, DECLARE, SUB

Points to note:

Variables that are declared as global in the main program can be used by the SUB, but variables that are declared as SHARED in the SUB are shared with the calling program only, not with any procedure called from the SUB itself unless they have been declared as SHARED in the SUB also. A parameter name cannot be declared as SHARED. As an example of sharing:

```
DECLARE SUB one (name$)     'procedure uses parameter
DECLARE SUB two ()          'put in by editor
a$ = "the test"             'assign string
CALL one(a$)                'call procedure and pass value
END

SUB one (name$)             'string passed as name$
PRINT name$                 'print to prove it
PRINT " is in SUB one"      'and show where
SHARED X$                   'new shared variable
X$ = name$                  'assigned with value
CALL two                    'call new procedure

END SUB

SUB two                     'called from SUB one
SHARED X$                   'confirm shared variable
PRINT X$                    'which has a value here
PRINT "is in SUB Two"       ' - prove it
END SUB
```

Beware of CALL statements in GWBasic or BASICA programs. These are equivalent to the CALL ABSOLUTE of QBASIC; they start a machine-code section of program running. If you need to run in QBASIC a program that was originally written for GWBasic or BASICA, change any CALL statements to CALL ABSOLUTE.

CALL ABSOLUTE

Type:	Statement
Typical syntax:	CALL ABSOLUTE address%
	CALL ABSOLUTE param%, address%
Action:	Transfers control to a machine-code routine (which should allow return to BASIC).
Options:	The address of an integer variable in the current data segment can be supplied as an integer parameter.
Argument(s):	Parameter address, address of machine-code routine in code segment
Restrictions:	None
Example:	

```
CALL ABSOLUTE (1024)   ' start machine code routine at 1024
```

Associated with: DEF SEG, VARPTR, VARPTR$

Points to note:

A thorough knowledge of machine code methods and use of PC memory is needed to make use of this command other than for examples printed in books and magazines. An incorrect address, either for the routine or for a parameter, can lead to the machine hanging up, requiring a reboot.

CASE

Type:	Statement
Typical syntax:	CASE number
	Action
	CASE number1, number2
	Action
	CASE number TO number
	Action
	CASE IS operator expression
	Action

Action: Allows a set of menu actions to be performed according to the value of a variable. Each CASE can be followed by a set of statement lines which will be performed if the CASE test returns a TRUE result.

Options: CASE ELSE allows for actions that will be triggered by anything that has not been tested by other CASE lines.

Argument(s): A single number or string; more than one number or string separated by commas, a range of numbers, or an expression using the symbols =, < >.

Restrictions: CASE can be used only in conjunction with SELECT. The form CASE IS *must* be used when a comparison operator (= < >) is present, and the = sign can be used for a normal selection, see example (b) below.

Examples:

(a)
```
SELECT CASE num%     'start - num% carries input number
   CASE 1            ' if num% is 1
      CALL tryone    'do this
   CASE 2 TO 5       ' if num% is 2 to 5
      CALL others    'do this
   CASE IS >= 6      ' if num% is 6 or more
      CALL tryagain  'do this
END CASE             ' marks end of block
```

(b)
```
DECLARE SUB savit ()        'these lines are
DECLARE SUB usit ()         'put in by the Editor
DECLARE SUB setitup ()      'when the file is saved
```

```
CLS
PRINT "please select by name -"
PRINT "setup, use, record, leave"    'list of possible
                                          replies
INPUT reply$                 'get as string variable
SELECT CASE reply$           'select by this
  CASE IS = "setup"          'first possible answer
    CALL setitup             'calls this
  CASE IS = "use"            'second one
    CALL usit                'call this
  CASE IS = "record"         'third one
    CALL savit               'calls this
  CASE ELSE                  'anything else
    PRINT "No choice made"   'no action
END SELECT                   'end of block

SUB savit                    'dummy routine
PRINT "Saving file"          'would use file save
END SUB                      'in this block

SUB setitup                  'another dummy
PRINT "Set up being done"    'routine for
END SUB                      'testing

SUB usit                     'last dummy
PRINT "Using routine"        'routine
END SUB
```

Associated with: IF...THEN...ELSE, ON...GOSUB, ON...GOTO, SELECT

Points to note:

SELECT and CASE offers very much more flexibility than the ON K% GOSUB type of menu choice, but for anything more than a simple set of number choices it is advisable to draw up a chart to show what action should be the result of each possible CASE choice. It is much easier to program for a range of values, and CASE ELSE allows for actions that are not catered for in other CASE lines. The variable that follows CASE in the SELECT CASE line can be a string, see example (b), allowing selection by letter or word rather than just by number – the use of CASE ELSE is essential in such a set of statements to avoid the effects of mis-spelling.

CDBL

Type:	Function returning a double-precision number
Typical syntax:	CDBL (number)
Action:	Converts a number or an expression into double-precision format. When any one variable in an expression is converted, the whole expression is worked out in double-precision.
Options:	None
Argument(s):	A number or expression to be converted into double-precision format and enclosed in brackets.
Restrictions:	The number must be within the double-precision range.

Example:

```
PRINT CDBL (1 / 11)    'will give result to 16 figures
A% = 3000              'assign
B% = 4000              'assign
C# = CDBL(A%) * B%     ' prevents overflow, see notes
```

Associated with: CINT, CLNG, CSNG

Points to note:

Converting a number into double-precision format does *not* make the number more precise unless the conversion acts on an expression that is capable of generating a number that is of double-precision. For example, using CDBL on a single-precision number variable does not increase the precision of that number, though using CDBL on a literal number will ensure that the number is stored in double-precision. By using CDBL on an expression that uses integers an overflow error can be avoided if, for example, a product of two integers works out to a number outside the integer range.

CHAIN

Type:	Statement
Typical syntax:	CHAIN filename
Action:	Loads and runs another QBASIC program.
Options:	None
Argument(s):	A valid filename of a QBASIC program, including the BAS extension.
Restrictions:	The new program will not be able to use any parameters from the calling program unless these have been declared as COMMON in *both* programs.

Example:

```
CHAIN C:\BASIC\FOLLOWON.BAS      'moves from present
                                  program to new
```

Associated with: CALL, COMMON, RUN

Points to note:

If the second program calls the first again, it will start the first program from the beginning – there is no option to start at a selected position in the program.

Programs written in earlier versions of BASIC that allow CHAIN to be followed by a line number should be rewritten to avoid this requirement.

If the chained program is to use variables whose values have been set by the calling program, these variables must be declared as COMMON in *both* programs, see entry for COMMON.

CHDIR

Type:	Statement
Typical syntax:	CHDIR directorypathname
Action:	Changes the current directory to the one nominated in the argument.
Options:	None
Argument(s):	Directory name as a string, literal or variable, with the full path if the directory is not a branch from the current directory.
Restrictions:	The abbreviation CD cannot be used as it is in MS-DOS. If the directory indicated in the argument does not exist, the *Path Not Found* error, number 76, will occur. The name must be within quotes or assigned to a string.

Example:

```
CHDIR "C:\TEXT\MYFILES"        'change to this directory
name$ = "C:\QBASIC\ALLFILES"   ' assign directory name
CHDIR name$                    ' change to this directory
```

Associated with: FILES, MKDIR, RMDIR

Points to note:

Changing the directory within a program also changes the directory that QBASIC is currently using. This could prevent you from loading in another program unless the directory is changed again.

CHR$

Type:	Function returning a string
Typical syntax:	string = CHR$(integer)
Action:	Returns a string consisting of the single character corresponding to the ASCII code (0 to 255) used as the argument.
Options:	None
Argument(s):	An ASCII code in the range 0 to 255, enclosed in brackets.
Restrictions:	The code number must be an integer – any number that is not an integer will be reduced to an integer. A number outside the range of 0 to 255 will cause an *Illegal Function Call* error, number 5.

Example:

```
FOR A% = 32 TO 127      'lower ASCII range
  PRINT CHR$(A%)        ' print character for number
NEXT                    ' complete loop
```

Associated with: ASC

Points to note:

Used mainly for obtaining characters that cannot be typed from the keyboard, such as the graphics characters. For making use of such characters in creating boxes, you can store the codes in a DATA line and use a loop such as:

```
READ ch%
FOR a% = 1 TO 80
  PRINT CHR$(ch%)
NEXT
```

to print a line of characters, reading other characters for other lines.

CINT

Type:	Function returning an integer
Typical syntax:	CINT(number)
Action:	Rounds a number or an expression to the nearest integer value.
Options:	None
Argument(s):	Any number or expression that produces a number in the integer range, enclosed in brackets.
Restrictions:	The range of argument must be -32768 to + 32767 only. An *Overflow* error, number 6, will occur for a number outside this range.

Example:

```
A% = CINT (B)
PRINT CINT (R * P + C)
```

Associated with: CDBL, CLNG, CSNG, FIX, INT

Points to note:

This action is performed automatically when an expression is assigned to an integer variable, so that CINT is normally required only in conjunction with PRINT.

CIRCLE

Type:	Statement
Typical syntax:	CIRCLE (centre) STEP, radius, colour, start, end, aspect.
Action:	Draws a circle, ellipse or part circle or ellipse on the screen.
Options:	STEP can be used before the radius figure to specify co-ordinates relative to the current position of the graphics cursor.
Argument(s):	Co-ordinates of centre of circle (default is current cursor position). The co-ordinates must be enclosed in brackets.
	Radius of circle (or average radius of ellipse).
	Colour number for boundary curve.
	Starting angle for arc (in radians) and ending angle for arc (in radians).
	Ratio of maximum X to maximum Y for ellipse (major/minor axis ratio).
	A comma is used to separate two arguments.
Restrictions:	If a colour argument is used it must be within the correct range for the screen type. Using an incorrect colour number produces an *Illegal Function Call* error, number 5. If intermediate arguments are omitted, their commas must be present.

Examples:

(a) Circle drawings

```
SCREEN 12                        'VGA in use
FOR N% = 10 TO 200 STEP 20       'set up numbers
   CIRCLE (320, 240), N%, 13     'set of blue circles
NEXT
```

(b) Arc drawings

```
SCREEN 12                         'VGA in use
COLOR 0                           'text colour
CIRCLE (127, 96), 80, 14, 0, 3.14 'draws yellow
                                   semi-circle
```

(c) Ellipse drawings

```
SCREEN 12                          'VGA in use
COLOR 0                            'text colour
CLS
FOR E = 1 TO .1 STEP -.1           'ellipticity numbers
   CIRCLE (320, 240), 100, 14, , , E  'note commas
NEXT                               'see results
SLEEP 1                            'wait
FOR E = 1 TO 3 STEP .2             'another lot
   CIRCLE (320, 240), 80, 15, , , E    ' over the first
NEXT
```

Associated with: COLOR, DRAW, LINE, PAINT, SCREEN, VIEW, WINDOW

Points to note:

The angles used as arguments for arc drawing must be in radians. If items such as the start and end of an arc are omitted, their commas must be put in place.

Negative angle values used for start and end will produce arcs with their ends connected to the centre (like a pie-chart segment). This does not work, however, with the value -0.

For converting degrees to radians, use a defined function of the form:

```
DEF degrad(ang) = ang * 3.1416 / 180
```

Closed circles and ellipses can be filled with colour by using the PAINT statement.

CLEAR

Type:	Statement
Typical syntax:	CLEAR
	CLEAR ,,stacksize
Action:	Clears variable memory by closing any open files, releasing file buffers, clearing all common variables, setting number variables and arrays to zero and string variables to null, and initialising the stack. Event trapping is also turned off. The stack size can be changed also, using an option.
Options:	Change the size of the stack
Argument(s):	None, optionally new stack size.
Restrictions:	The stack size must be of a value that can be supported. Do not change this unless you know what you are doing.

Example:

```
CLEAR ,,512  'clear memory and set stack of 512 bytes
REM commas are required
```

Associated with: ERASE

Points to note:

Use ERASE to clear arrays in the memory without clearing other variables. When the stack size is changed, the commas must be included, but do *not* place anything between the commas.

CLNG

Type:	Function returning long integer
Typical syntax:	variable = CLNG(expression)
Action:	Converts a number or number-expression into a long integer. Rounds fractions to the nearest whole number.
Options:	None
Argument(s):	Any number, variable or expression whose value, when rounded, falls within the long integer range. The argument must be enclosed in brackets.
Restrictions:	The argument must be within the range of a long integer, which is the range of -2,147,483,648 to +2,147,483,647

Examples:

```
PRINT CLNG(A% * B% + C)
PRINT CLNG(3.1E6)
```

Associated with: CDBL, CINT, CSNG, FIX, INT

Points to note:

An *Overflow* error, number 6, occurs if the number argument is out of the long integer range.

CLOSE

Type:	Statement
Typical syntax:	CLOSE filenumber
Action:	Closes a specified open file (or device), or all open files or devices.
Options:	Can be used with no argument to close all open files, or to close more than one nominated file using CLOSE #1, #2, #3, etc.
Argument(s):	Channel number of an open file or an open device (such as PRN or CON).
Restrictions:	None

Example:

```
OPEN "myfile" FOR INPUT AS #1      'open sequential 1
OPEN "newfile" FOR OUTPUT AS #2    'open sequential 2
OPEN "oldfile" FOR BINARY AS #3    'open binary 3
OPEN "PRN:" FOR OUTPUT AS #4       'printer is #4
...................                'other statements
CLOSE #1                           'close sequential 1
...................                'other statements
CLOSE                              'close all files
```

Associated with: END, OPEN, RESET, STOP

Points to note:

Using CLOSE ensures that all buffers are written (flushed) before closing. This is a useful way of ensuring that all file data is written to the disk and that the MS-DOS directory will be updated. Note that END, RESET, RUN and STOP also close all open files and devices.

CLS

Type:	Statement
Typical syntax:	CLS
	CLS 0 or CLS 1 or CLS2
Action:	Clears the whole screen or a selected window and places the cursor at the top left hand corner of the screen or selected window.
Options:	The number argument need not be used if no separate windows are in use.
Argument(s):	0, 1 or 2 depending on use of viewing windows. CLS used alone clears any graphics window. If there are no graphics windows, but there is a text window, CLS clears the text window. If no windows are in use CLS clears the screen or text and/or graphics.

As used with arguments:

CLS 0 Clears the entire screen of text and graphics.
CLS 1 Clears the graphics window (if there is no graphics window in use, clears the whole screen)
CLS2 Clears the text window.

Restrictions:	None
Example:	

```
CLS
T$ = "TITLE"
GOSUB Printcentre
```

Associated with: VIEW, VIEW PRINT, WINDOW

Points to note:

Programs should always start with CLS, because the Results screen of QBASIC retains text and graphics from previous programs until a CLS is issued or until another piece of software replaces the QBASIC interpreter.

COLOR

Type:	Statement
Typical syntax:	COLOR foreground, background, border (text screen 0)
	COLOR background, palette (low-resolution screen 1)
	COLOR foreground (VGA high-resolution screen 4, 12, 13)
	COLOR foreground, background (screen 7 to 10)
Action:	Sets colours for foreground, background and border for text screen and for default foreground for VGA high-resolution graphics screen.
Options:	Depend on screen mode in use.
Argument(s):	Foreground, palette, background, border colour numbers, depending on screen mode in use. Any argument can be omitted providing any preceding comma is included.

SCREEN number	Graphics resolution	Arguments
0 (Text screen)	————	foreground, background, border
1 (CGA,EGA,VGA,MCGA)	320 x 200	background, palette
12 (VGA)	640 x 480	foreground
13 (VGA or MGCA)	320 x 200	foreground
7 (EGA or VGA)	320 x 200	foreground, background
8 (EGA or VGA)	640 x 200	foreground, background
9 (EGA or VGA)	640 x 350	foreground, background
10 (EGA or VGA Mono)	640 x 350	foreground, background

For SCREEN 1, the palette numbers that can be used are 0 or 1, and each switches in a set of colours for three different attribute numbers:

palette number	1	2	3
0	Green	Red	Brown
1	Cyan	Magenta	Bright white

For a VGA type of graphics board, the available colours are determined by the PALETTE statement.

The standard colour code numbers are:

0	Black	1	Blue	2	Green
3	Cyan	4	Red	5	Magenta
6	Brown	7	White	8	Gray

9	Light blue	10	Light green	11	Light cyan
12	Light red	13	Light magenta	14	Yellow
15	Bright white				

Note: Cyan is the mixture of Blue and Green light

Magenta is the mixture of Blue and Red light

Yellow is the mixture of Green and Red light

Restrictions: The border option is used on text screens only. The numbers that can be used depend on the selected screen mode and the use of PALETTE for choice of colours. The foreground colour is used for text on all textscreens. For monochrome monitors, colour numbers 0 to 31 are interpreted differently:

0	Black	16	Black
1	White underline	17	Black underline
2-7	White	18-23	Flashing
8	Black	24	Black
9	Bright underline	25	Bright flashing underline
10-15	Bright white	26-31	Bright flashing

Examples:

```
COLOR 14    'Sets yellow foreground for 640 x 480 VGA

REM example for VGA screen
SCREEN 12    'set VGA 640 x 460 screen mode
CLS          'establish screen
FOR col% = 0 TO 15
  COLOR col%
  PRINT "Colour"; col%
NEXT
```

Associated with: DRAW, PAINT, PALETTE, PALETTE USING, SCREEN

Points to note:

The required syntax depends on the screen mode that is being used. For modern machines, options for CGA and EGA can be ignored, since virtually all modern machines use VGA screen cards. QBASIC is not able to make full use of the colour possibilities of modern VGA cards, and certainly not of SVGA.

COM

Type:	Statement
Typical syntax:	COM (number) ON
	COM (number) OFF
	COM (number) STOP
	ON COM (number) GOSUB subname
Action:	COM ON enables trapping of a serial communications port input.
	COM OFF disables trapping and COM STOP suspends trapping. When COM ON has been used, ON COM GOSUB will run the specified subroutine when there is an input at the serial port.
Options:	None
Argument(s):	A COM port number in range 1 to 4, usually 1 or 2.
Restrictions:	The serial communications port must be physically present and connected to a modem or to another computer or some other source of signals.

Examples:

(a) Report input only

```
COM(2) ON                       'My COM1 is used by mouse
ON COM (2) GOSUB readport       'routine for COM2
PRINT "Press any key to stop"   'how to escape
DO WHILE INKEY$ = ""            'start loop
LOOP                            'until event or key pressed
COM(2) OFF                      'end trapping

readport:                       'detect
PRINT "Message received"        'character at port
RETURN                          'but do not read it
```

(b) Prints received file

```
ON COM(2) GOSUB getinput        'use COM2
COM(2) ON                       'activate
OPEN "com2:" FOR RANDOM AS #1   'open
DO WHILE INKEY$ = ""            'infinite
PRINT combuf$                   'loop
```

```
LOOP                          'until key or message
END

getinput:                     'COM routine
INPUT #1, combuf$             'get a line
RETURN                        'that's all
```

Associated with: OPEN COM

Points to note:

This provides QBASIC with the basis of statements to write communications programs. This should not be attempted unless you are familiar with the use of serial ports and serial protocols. In general, each input from a COM port can be read in as a character, using GET, into a string array, with the subscript number incremented each time a character is received. In example (b) above, INPUT #1 has been used to read the incoming file one line at a time and print each line as it is received.

The OPEN COM statement is needed to set up the COM port (the default baudrate is 300) and for modern use you are more likely to require 2400 or higher. Note that for reading one character at a time you can use LEN = 1 at the end of the OPEN COM statement.

COMMON

Type:	Statement
Typical syntax:	COMMON variable list
	COMMON SHARED variable list
Action:	Defines a list of global variables that can be used by a chained (see CHAIN) program and optionally by all subroutines.
Options:	SHARED to indicate that all SUB and FUNCTION routines will make use of the variables.
Argument(s):	A list of variables to be declared as COMMON.
Restrictions:	A variable can be declared as COMMON only once, though a program can contain more than one COMMON statement.
	COMMON and DECLARE lines must be placed ahead of any executable (action) statements of a program.

Example:

```
COMMON name AS STRING        'Equivalent to using name$

COMMON numlist() AS INTEGER 'Array of integers declaration
```

The following pair of program examples demonstrate the use of COMMON in chaining programs. Save the second program as SECOND.BAS and run the first.

```
(a)  REM Main program
     COMMON a, b$ ' This makes a and b$ common to both programs
     CLS
     a = 6.667    ' assign value
     b$ = "Example"  ' assign value
     PRINT a, b$; " exist in main program"
     SLEEP 5       'wait
     CHAIN "SECOND.BAS" ' chain in second program
     END
```

(b)
```
REM Second program
COMMON a, b$    ' need to repeat declaration here
x = 2 * a ' check that variable a exists
C$ = "New " + b$   ' check that variable b$ exists
PRINT C$, x; " in second program"
END
```

Associated with: CHAIN, DIM, REDIM, FUNCTION, SHARED,
STATIC, SUB

Points to note:

Unless otherwise declared in an earlier DIM statement, any array declared in a COMMON statement is a dynamic array, see Appendix B. When COMMON is used to make a variable retain its value when another program is chained (see CHAIN), there must be a matching COMMON statement in the CHAINED program, as shown in the example above.

CONST

Type: Statement

Typical syntax: CONST name = assignment

Action: Sets a name to represent a number or string which will not be changed in the course of a program.

Options: None

Argument(s): A number, expression or string.

Restrictions: The assigned quantity must not use the exponentiation sign. Any attempt to re-assign a constant will cause an error.

Examples:

(a)
```
CONST PI = 3.1416
PRINT "1 radian is "; 180/PI; " degrees"
```

(b)
```
CONST hisname = "J. MacGregor", hisnum = 22416
PRINT hisname; " number ";hisnum
```

Associated with: INTEGER, LONG, SINGLE, DOUBLE, STRING

Points to note:

Using a CONST type for numbers such as PI avoids any risk that the value could be changed by an unintended re-assignment, as can happen when a variable is used.

Older versions of BASIC do not possess the CONST type, and use a variable to retain these quantities. This is perfectly satisfactory for running under QBASIC, but a QBASIC program that contains a CONST declaration cannot run under a version of BASIC that does not support CONST.

COS

Type:	Function returning double-precision number
Typical syntax:	COS (angle)
Action:	Returns the cosine (see Appendix A) of the angle, measured in radians, which is used as an argument.
Options:	None
Argument(s):	The angle in units of radians as a number, variable or expression, within brackets.
Restrictions:	The argument is an angle in radians. Use A * PI / 180 for angle A in degrees, with PI defined as 3.1416.

Example:

```
SIDE = HYPOT * COS(angle)   ' find length of side

CONST PI = 3.1416           ' for conversion
FOR ang% = 5 TO 85 STEP 5   ' prints a table of cosines
   PRINT" Angle"; ang%; "    Cosine ";COS(ang% * PI / 180)
NEXT
```

Associated with: ATN, SIN, TAN

Points to note:

Very small angles give unreliable results, as do angles which are close to 90° or multiples of 90° (any multiple of PI/2 radians). The conversions between radians and degrees should be carried out using defined functions. The value of PI should be taken as 3.1416 unless high precision is needed.

CSNG

Type:	Function returning single-precision number
Typical syntax:	PRINT CSNG(A%/B%)
Action:	Converts the argument into single-precision form.
Options:	None
Argument(s):	Any number or expression that will result in a number, enclosed within brackets.
Restrictions:	The results must not exceed the limits of a single-precision number.

Example:

```
A = CSNG(D#)
REM converts the double-precision number D# into
REM single-precision form as variable A.
```

Associated with: CDBL, CINT, CLNG

Points to note:

CSNG is used mainly to prevent overflow during the processing of integer variables. For example, the multiplication of two integers can result in a number that is outside the integer range, and using CSNG on either variable will ensure that all processing is carried out in single-precision arithmetic.

Conversion of a higher precision number to a lower precision may cause small errors that can cause trouble if they accumulate to a total.

CSRLIN

Type:	Function returning integer number
Typical syntax:	varname = CSRLIN
Action:	Returns a number for the row in which the cursor is currently located.
Options:	None
Argument(s):	None
Restrictions:	The row number is an integer in the range 1 to 25

Example:

```
X% = CSRLIN              ' store position of current line
LOCATE X%, 10            ' put cursor to row 10, same line
PRINT "Position here" ' print at this position
```

Associated with: LOCATE, POS, VIEW PRINT

Points to note:

CSRLN and POS provide a way of storing a cursor position for use later if a screen position needs to be recalled after clearing it. They are particularly useful along with LOCATE if separate screen windows are being used, allowing the cursor to be switched from one window to another into the position it previously occupied.

CVI

Type:	Function returning integer
Typical syntax:	integer variable = CVI (string)
Action:	Converts a two-byte string that was created using MKI$ back into an integer number.
Options:	None
Argument(s):	A two-character string used to encode a number, created by MKI$, enclosed within brackets.
Restrictions:	Used only in the older type of file records. Modern programs should declare user defined variable (a *record* variable) rather than using these conversions.

Example:

```
A% = 65                              'assign integer
B% = 16706                           'variables A% and B%
A$ = MKI$(A%)                        'make string of A%
PRINT A$; "    ("; LEN(A$); ")"      'Print to demonstrate
B$ = MKI$(B%)                        'same for
PRINT B$; "    ("; LEN(B$); ")"      'B%
PRINT CVI(A$); "  "; CVI(B$)         'converts back and print
```

Associated with: CVD, CVDMBF, CVL, CVS, CVSMBF, FIELD, MKD$, MKDMBF$, MKI$, MKL$, MKS$, MKSMBF$

Points to note:

The string created in this way is not the same as would be created using STR$, but consists of the characters equivalent to the pair of bytes used to encode the integer. For example, the integer 16448 is encoded as byte values 64 and 65 (because 64 x 256 + 65 = 16448), and these as characters are AB. Using STR$ would require six characters (one for each digit, plus a space). Using MKI$ allows all integers to be stored in a random-access file as two bytes each.

CVI is intended for maintenance purposes to ensure compatibility with older programs. New programs should defined a user type to hold the numbers and strings that will be used in a random access file.

CVD

Type:	Function returning double-precision number
Typical syntax:	double-precision variable = CVD (string)
Action:	Converts an eight-character string created by using MKD$ to a double-precision number.
Options:	None
Argument(s):	An eight-byte string created by using MKD$ on a double-precision number, enclosed in brackets.
Restrictions:	Used only in the older type of file records. Modern programs should declare a user-defined variable (a *record* variable) rather than using these conversions.

Example:

```
D# = 216.45169#              'assign number
D$ = MKD$(D#)                'convert to string
PRINT D$; "    ("; LEN(D$); ")"   'print string and length
PRINT CVD(D$)                'convert back
```

Associated with: CVDMBF, CVSMBF, CVI, CVL, CVS, FIELD, MKD$, MKDMBF$, MKI$, MKL$, MKS$, MKSMBF$

Points to note:

The string created in this way is not the same as would be created using STR$, but consists of the characters equivalent to the eight bytes used to encode a double-precision number of any size. Using STR$ would require one character for each digit, plus a space. Using MKD$ allows all double-precision numbers to be stored in a random-access file as eight bytes each.

CVD is intended for maintenance purposes to ensure compatibility with older programs. New programs should defined a user type to hold the numbers and strings that will be used in a random access file.

QBASIC uses floating point (single and double) numbers in IEEE form, and this affects the coded version produced by MKD$. Older versions of BASIC used another format, Microsoft Binary Format, and to ensure correct conversion of random-access file data from old files, the CVDMBF function should be used. Similarly, in adding data to old files, the MKDMBF$ function must be used to ensure compatibility. It is preferable to use these routines only in a short program that will open the old file and also open a new file, reading from the old file using CVDMBF and CVSMBF and writing to the new one using a user-defined record type.

CVDMBF

Type:	Function returning double-precision number
Typical syntax:	double precision variable = CVDMBF (string)
Action:	Converts an eight-character string in Microsoft Binary format into a double-precision number in IEEE standard format as used by QBASIC.
Options:	None
Argument(s):	An eight-byte string created by using MKDMBF$ in QBASIC, or by using MKD$ in an earlier version of BASIC. The argument must be enclosed in brackets.
Restrictions:	Used only for maintenance of random-access files that were created by an older version of BASIC using Microsoft Binary format for floating-point numbers. The example shows the outline of a system for converting old random-access files into new ones.

Example:

```
GOSUB openfile          'open old random file
GET #file%, data%       'get string from file
amount# = CVDMBF (cash$) 'convert a number
PRINT amount#           'and print it
GOSUB newfile           'save to new file using
                        'modern QBASIC statements
```

Associated with: CVD, CVDMBF, CVI, CVL, CVS, CVSMBF, FIELD, MKD$, MKDMBF$, MKI$, MKL$, MKS$, MKSMBF$

Points to note:

QBASIC uses floating point (single and double) numbers in IEEE form, and this affects the coded version produced by MKD$. Older versions of BASIC used another format, Microsoft Binary Format, and to ensure correct conversion of random-access file data from old files, the CVDMBF function should be used. Similarly, in adding data to old files, the MKDMBF$ function must be used to ensure compatibility. It is preferable to use these routines only in a short program that will open the old file and also open a new file, reading from the old file using CVDMBF and CVSMBF and writing to the new one using a user-defined record type.

CVL

Type:	Function
Typical syntax:	long integer variable = CVL (string)
Action:	Converts a four-character string that was created by using MKL$ into a long integer number.
Options:	None
Argument(s):	A four-byte string created using MKL$ on a long integer number and enclosed in brackets.
Restrictions:	CVL must not be used on a four-byte string that was created using MKS$.

Example:

```
S& = 125712                          'assign long integer
long$ = MKL$(S&)                     'convert
PRINT long$; " ("; LEN(long$); ")"   'print string and length
PRINT "Value is "; CVL(long$)        'convert back and print
```

Associated with: CVD, CVI, CVS, FIELD, MKD$, MKI$, MKL$, MKS$

Points to note:

Older versions of interpreted PC BASIC did not use the long-integer type, but compiled BASIC versions did. Some versions of BASIC for other machines also used long integers – the BBC micro, for example, used this format in 1981. The string created in this way is not the same as would be created using STR$, but consists of the characters equivalent to the set of four bytes used to encode the long integer. Using STR$ would require one character for each digit, plus a space. Using MKL$ allows all long integers to be stored in a random-access file as four bytes each.

CVL is intended for maintenance purposes to ensure compatibility with older programs. New programs should define a user type to hold the numbers and strings that will be used in a random access file.

CVS

Type:	Function returning single-precision number
Typical syntax:	single-precision variable = CVS (string)
Action:	Converts a four-character string that was created using MKS$ into a single precision number.
Options:	None
Argument(s):	four-byte string created using MKS$ on a single precision number and enclosed in brackets.
Restrictions:	Used only in the older type of file records. Modern programs should declare user-defined variable (a *record* variable) rather than using these conversions.

Example:

```
X = 22.45                            'assign single
X$ = MKS$(X)                         'convert
PRINT X$; "  ("; LEN(X$); ")"        'print string and length
Print CVS (X$)                       'convert back
```

Associated with: CVD, CVDMBF, CVI, CVL, CVSMBF, FIELD, MKD$, MKDMBF$, MKI$, MKL$, MKS$, MKSMBF$

Points to note:

The string created in this way is not the same as would be created using STR$, but consists of the characters equivalent to the four bytes used to encode a single-precision number of any permitted size. Using STR$ would require one character for each digit, plus a space. Using MKS$ allows all single-precision numbers to be stored in a random-access file as four bytes each.

CVS is intended for maintenance purposes to ensure compatibility with older programs. New programs should defined a user type to hold the numbers and strings that will be used in a random access file.

QBASIC uses floating point (single and double) numbers in IEEE form, and this affects the coded version produced by MKS$. Older versions of BASIC used another format, Microsoft Binary Format, and to ensure correct conversion of random-access file data from old files, the CVSMBF function should be used. Similarly, in adding data to old files, the MKSMBF$ function must be used to ensure compatibility. It is preferable to use these routines only in a short program that will open the old file and also open a new file, reading from the old file using CVDMBF and CVSMBF and writing to the new one using a user-defined record type.

CVSMBF

Type:	Function returning single-precision number
Typical syntax:	single-precision variable = CVSMBF (string)
Action:	Converts a four-character string in Microsoft Binary Format into a single precision number in IEEE format as used by QBASIC.
Options:	None
Argument(s):	A four-byte string created by using MKSMBF$ on an IEEE format number, or by using MKS$ on an older version of BASIC. The argument must be enclosed in brackets.
Restrictions:	Used only for maintenance of random-access files that were created by an older version of BASIC using Microsoft Binary format for floating point numbers. The example shows the outline of a system for converting old random-access files into new ones.

Example:

```
GOSUB openfile           'open old random file
GET #file%, data%        'get string from file
amount! = CVSMBF (cash$) 'convert a number
PRINT amount!            'and print it
GOSUB newfile            'save to new file using
                         'modern QBASIC statements
```

Associated with: CVDMBF, FIELD, MKDMBF$, MKSMBF$

Points to note:

QBASIC uses floating point (single and double) numbers in IEEE form, and this affects the coded version produced by MKS$. Older versions of BASIC used another format, Microsoft Binary Format, and to ensure correct conversion of random-access file data from old files, the CVSMBF function should be used. Similarly, in adding data to old files, them MKSMBF$ function must be used to ensure compatibility. It is preferable to use these routines only in a short program that will open the old file and also open a new file, reading from the old file using CVDMBF and CVSMBF and writing to the new one using a user-defined record type.

DATA

Type:	Statement
Typical syntax:	DATA item, item,…
Action:	Marks a list of values to be used by a READ statement, usually to be assigned to variables.
Options:	None.
Argument(s):	None.
Restrictions:	The items can be number or string, but only a number item can be read into a number variable. A *Type mismatch error*, Error 13, will occur if a string item is read into a number variable. To ensure that all items can be read, use a string variable, and for an array or matrix use a string array unless you are certain that all items are numbers.

Example:

```
FOR j% = 1 TO 3          'three sets
FOR k % = 1 TO 2         'two items each
READ mat$(j%, k%)        'read as strings
NEXT: NEXT               'complete loops
SLEEP 1                  'wait
CLS
FOR j% = 1 TO 3          'read back
FOR k% = 1 TO 2          'matrix
PRINT mat$(j%, k%)       'print values
NEXT: NEXT
DATA John. K. Quinn,1, "Andrews, W.K.",56, T. P. Quinn,78
END
REM You can READ a set of numbers as strings, but
REM you cannot read strings as numbers.
REM Use VAL if you need to work with numbers.
```

Associated with: READ, RESTORE

Points to note:

If a string constant contains a comma, the whole string must be surrounded by quotes, otherwise the comma will be taken as the divider between two DATA items. It is an error to read data that does not exist

(Out of Data, Error 4), but there is no error in having data unread.

The use of READ...DATA for providing values that will be used throughout a program is a relict of old BASIC methods. Where constants are to be used, QBASIC provides the CONST statement. READ...DATA is, however, useful for filling an array of values, particularly for testing a program. It also allows the program to be written and values decided on later.

DATE$ function

Type:	Function returning string
Typical syntax:	PRINT DATE$
Action:	Returns a 10-character string containing the current date.
Options:	None.
Argument(s):	None.
Restrictions:	The year used in DATE$ must be in the range 1980 to 2099 The date format is U.S. with month number, day number and year number in that order.
Example:	`A$ = DATE$`
	`PRINT DATE$`

Associated with: DATE$ (statement), TIME$

Points to note:

The date is obtained from the computer's own clock system. Computer clocks are notoriously inaccurate (because of interruptions to the system by the mouse and other attachments) and though they are seldom as much as a day out, the time of midnight can be quite far out from its true time. If you make use of DATE$ in programming, correct the computer clock at least once a week (see DATE$ statement). The original PC machine had to have the date and time set each time it was switched on, so that this problem did not become a nuisance until the development of machines with built-in clocks and CMOS memory.

There is no option to print DATE$ in any format other than the month-day-year U.S. system.

DATE$ statement

Type:	Statement
Typical syntax:	DATE$ = string
Action:	Sets the computer current date to the date in the supplied 10-character string.
Options:	None.
Argument(s):	None
Restrictions:	The date must be expressed in the string as any of the forms: mm-dd-yy, mm-dd-yyyy, mm/dd/yy, mm/dd/yyyy; all using the month number as the first item. The earliest year you can use is 1980 and the latest is 2099.
Example:	**DATE$ = "10-10-93"**
	PRINT DATE$

Associated with: DATE$ (function), TIME$

Points to note:

Using the DATE$ statement to alter the date setting will also alter the date setting for the computer as a whole. If this might be a problem, for example if your BASIC program is concerned with generating a calendar for a year in the future, you can save the current date as another variable, using NOW$ = DATE$, and at the end of your program restore the current date by using DATE$ = NOW$.

See also under DATE$ function.

DECLARE

Type:	Statement.
Typical syntax:	DECLARE FUNCTION name (parameters)
	DECLARE SUB name (parameters)
Action:	Used to declare a FUNCTION or SUB procedure.
Options:	None.
Argument(s):	Parameter list, if applicable. Parameters must be separated by commas.
Restrictions:	Parameters will be checked for correct type, unless ANY has been used. If no DECLARE lines have been written, the Editor will supply them when a program is saved. Such automatically created DECLARE lines will be of a simple format with no *name AS type* lines. There must be no executable program lines ahead of a DECLARE line – all DECLARE and COMMON statement lines must be at the start of the program. If DECLARE lines are generated automatically by the Editor they will be placed at the start of the program.

Examples:

(a)
```
DECLARE FUNCTION Count (num AS INTEGER, Mon AS SINGLE)
REM This declares a function called Count which will
REM take two parameters, an integer and a single-precision
REM in that order. The parameters that are used to call
REM the function as, for example:
REM             Count (27, 12.75)
REM will be checked to ensure that they are of the
REM correct types.
```

(b)
```
DECLARE SUB Maintain (ManyData AS ANY, Array() AS STRING
REM This declares a Procedure called Maintain which can
REM take as its first parameter any data type, followed
REM by a string array
```

(c)
```
DECLARE SUB demo ()        'created by editor
CLS
DIM SHARED n%             'all variables old-fashioned type
n% = 10
```

```
CALL demo
PRINT "a% outside is"; a% 'no values assigned
PRINT "b% outside is"; b% 'outside the SUB
END

SUB demo
  a% = 2 * n%                'local values
  b% = 3 * n%                'exist only inside SUB demo
  PRINT "a% inside is"; a%
  PRINT "b% inside is"; b%
END SUB
```

(d)
```
DECLARE FUNCTION geteqn! (a!, b!, c!) 'put in by editor
CLS
a = 2.5                      'assign values
b = 5.4
c = 2.2
y = geteqn(a, b, c)          'call function
PRINT "Y is"; y              'print result
END

FUNCTION geteqn (a, b, c)    'header
geteqn = a ^ 2 + 6 * b + c   'action
END FUNCTION                 'end marker
```

Associated with: CALL, FUNCTION, SUB

Points to note:

A variable declared as being of type ANY will *not* be checked for type before the procedure starts – if the type is wrong the program will halt with an error message. If a normal type is specified this will be checked before the procedure or function runs.

DEF FN

Type: Statement.

Typical syntax:
DEF FNname(parameters) = expression
REM Single-line version
DEF FNname(parameters)
    Statement
    Statement
    FNname = expression
END DEF
REM Multi-line version

Action: Defines a function which will be called by using FNname at some point in the program. Optional parameters can be passed to the function and one value can be passed back.

Options: The Function Definition can consist of a single line, or multiple lines terminated by END DEF.

Argument(s): The parameters, if required, to be passed to the function. The parameters can also define variable types, using name AS type (see also DECLARE). Parameters must be enclosed in brackets.

Restrictions: Only one parameter value can be passed back by way of the FNname = expression line.

If a defined function returns a string its name *must* be a string name, ending with the dollar sign.

All variable names used inside a defined function are local to the function; they have no value or meaning outside the function.

Examples:

(a)
```
DEF FNsumofsq(a, b) = SQR(a ^ 2 + b ^ 2)    'definition
PRINT FNsumofsq(3, 4)                        'use with PRINT
X% = FNsumofsq(12, 13)                       'assignment
PRINT X%                                     'print value
```

(b)
```
DEF FNbitofstring$ (A$, n%) = UCASE$(LEFT$(A$, n%))
REM Note the string name for a string function
CLS
A$ = "this is a test string"
```

```
      FOR n% = 1 TO LEN(A$)
      PRINT FNbitofstring$(A$, n%)          'using function
      NEXT
```

(c)
```
      CLS
      CONST rad = 180 / 3.1416
      INPUT "X and Y values"; a, b   'cartesian values
      DEF fncarpol (x, y)            'converts to polar
        lg = SQR(x ^ 2 + y ^ 2)       'length
        theta = ATN(y / x) * rad      'angle
        PRINT "Size is "; lg          'print length
        PRINT "Angle is "; theta; " degrees"  'print angle
      END DEF
      x = FNcarpol(a, b)             'call function
      REM Function is called using dummy variable x
      REM because a function needs to be called somehow and
      REM using PRINT FNcarpol(a, b) is not appropriate
```

Associated with: END DEF, EXIT, FUNCTION, SHARED, STATIC

Points to note:

All variables used in a defined function are local, unless they are defined as SHARED. Variables declared as STATIC will also be local, but will resume their values the next time the function is called.

This is an older type of statement, now superseded by FUNCTION, though the multi-line form of DEF FN is easy to use and much more flexible than the older type.

One point to be careful about regards case of letters. Normally if you type reserved words of QBASIC in lower-case they are converted to uppercase when you press the ENTER key or move to the next line, so that, for example, print is converted to PRINT. This is a useful way of checking that a keyword has been spelled correctly and spaced correctly from words ahead or following.

This does not happen when FN is used, because FN is always joined to the name of the function, as, for example, FNsumofsq, FNequation. More care therefore needs to be taken with the FN part of a DEF FN function than with other reserved words.

DEF SEG

Type: Statement.

Typical syntax: DEF SEG (address number)

Action: Sets the current memory segment to be either the current data segment or the segment whose address number is supplied.

Options: Can be used with or without parameter.

Argument(s):   Segment address number.

Restrictions: If a segment address number is supplied it must be in the range 0 to 65535, hex &H0000 to &HFFFF.

Examples:

```
DEF SEG       'sets current data segment
DEF SEG = 0   'sets current segment as first 64 Kb of RAM
```

Associated with: BLOAD, BSAVE, CALL ABSOLUTE, PEEK, POKE, VARPTR, VARPTR$

Points to note:

This is a memory-setting statement that should be used only by programmers who are well acquainted with the memory structure of the PC machine. See Appendix C for notes on segmented addressing. Using the wrong segment along with a statement that writes to memory (such as POKE) or sets a program running (such as CALL ABSOLUTE) can lock up the machine, requiring a reboot.

DEFDBL

Type:	Statement.
Typical syntax:	DEFDBL (list)
Action:	Sets initial letters of names to be used as default double-precision number type.
Options:	None
Argument(s):	A single letter, list of letters or letter range, enclosed in brackets.
Restrictions:	Upper and lower case letters are treated as identical.

Examples:

(a)
```
DEFDBL (A)
REM All names starting with A are double-precision
REM number variables
Alex$ = "Bellus perennis"
REM Over-ridden by specific case using $
```

(b)
```
DEFDBL (A,J,S)
REM All names starting with these letters are
REM double-precision variables.
```

(c)
```
DEFDBL REM (A - K)
REM All names starting with letters
REM from A to K are double-precision variables
```

Associated with: DEFINT, DEFLNG, DEFSNG, DEFSTR

Points to note:

This default can be over-ridden by using a normal variable suffix, such as ASTM$ or ASHES%, or by the use of a declaration using, for example, Atitle AS INTEGER. When a DEF type of declaration of a variable has been made, each SUB procedure created by QBASIC will automatically contain a repeat declaration.

The use of defaults can avoid the use of the normal suffixes (!,#,%,&,$) but at the expense of making a reader of the program listing continually need to refer back to find what type is being used. It is particularly irritating if several variables over-ride the defaults.

DEFINT

Type: Statement.

Typical syntax: DEFINT (list).

Action: Sets initial letters of names to be used as default integer number type.

Options: None.

Argument(s): A single letter, list of letters or letter range, enclosed in brackets.

Restrictions: Upper and lower case letters are treated as identical.

Examples:

(a)
```
DEFINT (A)
REM All names starting with A are integer
REM number variables
Ajax! = 21.776 'over-rides default
```

(b)
```
DEFINT (A,J,S)
REM All names starting with these letters are
REM integer variables
```

(c)
```
DEFINT (A - K)
REM All names starting with letters from A to K
REM are integer variables
```

Associated with: DEFDBL, DEFLNG, DEFSNG, DEFSTR

Points to note:

This default can be over-ridden by using a normal variable suffix, such as ASTM$ or ASHES#, or by the use of a declaration using, for example, Atitle AS STRING. When a DEF type of declaration of a variable has been made, each SUB procedure created by QBASIC will automatically contain a repeat declaration.

The use of defaults can avoid the use of the normal suffixes (!,#,%,&,$) but at the expense of making a reader of the program listing continually need to refer back to find what type is being used. It is particularly irritating if several variables over-ride the defaults.

DEFLNG

Type:	Statement.
Typical syntax:	DEFLNG (list).
Action:	Sets initial letters of names to be used as default long-integer number type.
Options:	None.
Argument(s):	Single letter, list of letters or letter range, enclosed in brackets.
Restrictions:	Upper and lower case letters are treated as identical.

Examples:

(a) `DEFLNG (A)`

```
REM All names starting with A are long-integer number
REM variables
Arch% = 56    'Over-ride default
```

(b) `DEFLNG (A,J,S)`

```
REM All names starting with these letters are
REM long-integer variables
```

(c) `DEFLNG (A - K)`

```
REM All names starting with letters from A to K
REM are long-integer variables
```

Associated with: DEFDBL, DEFINT, DEFSNG, DEFSTR

Points to note:

This default can be over-ridden by using a normal variable suffix, such as ASTM$ or ASHES%, or by the use of a declaration using, for example, Atitle AS INTEGER. The long integer type is not used on older versions of interpreted BASIC. When a DEF type of declaration of a variable has been made, each SUB procedure created by QBASIC will automatically contain a repeat declaration.

The use of defaults can avoid the use of the normal suffixes (!,#,%,&,$) but at the expense of making a reader of the program listing continually need to refer back to find what type is being used. It is particularly irritating if several variables over-ride the defaults.

Note that older versions of BASIC (other than compiled types) did not permit use of long integers so that this statement did not exist.

DEFSNG

Type:	Statement.
Typical syntax:	DEFSNG (list).
Action:	Sets initial letters of names to be used as default single-precision number type.
Options:	None.
Argument(s):	A single letter, list of letters or letter range, enclosed in brackets.
Restrictions:	Upper and lower case letters are treated as identical.

Examples:

(a) `DEFSNG (A)`

```
REM All names starting with A are single-precision number
REM variables
Artful$ = "Degas"    'Over-rides default
```

(b) `DEFSNG (A,J,S)`

```
REM All names starting with these letters are
REM single-precision variables.
```

(c) `DEFSNG (A - K)`

```
REM All names starting with letters from A to K are
REM single precision variables
```

Associated with: DEFDBL, DEFINT, DEFLNG, DEFSTR

Points to note:

This default can be over-ridden by using a normal variable suffix, such as ASTM$ or ASHES%, or by the use of a declaration using, for example, Atitle AS INTEGER. When a DEF type of declaration of a variable has been made, each SUB procedure created by QBASIC will automatically contain a repeat declaration.

The use of defaults can avoid the use of the normal suffixes (!,#,%,&,$) but at the expense of making a reader of the program listing continually need to refer back to find what type is being used. It is particularly irritating if several variables over-ride the defaults.

DEFSTR

Type:	Statement.
Typical syntax:	DEFSTR (list).
Action:	Sets initial letters of names to be used as default string variable type.
Options:	None.
Argument(s):	A single letter, list of letters or letter range, enclosed in brackets.
Restrictions:	Upper and lower case letters are treated as identical.

Examples:

(a)
```
DEFSTR (A)
REM All names starting with A are string variables.
Ashes# = 33.116782 'Over-rides default
```

(b)
```
DEFSTR (A,J,S)
REM All names starting with these letters are
REM string variables.
```

(c)
```
DEFSTR (A - K)
REM All names starting with letters from A to K are
REM string variables.
```

Associated with: DEFINT, DEFLNG, DEFSNG, DEFSTR

Points to note:

This default can be over-ridden by using a normal variable suffix, such as ASTM# or ASHES%, or by the use of a declaration using, for example, Atitle AS INTEGER. When a DEF type of declaration of a variable has been made, each SUB procedure created by QBASIC will automatically contain a repeat declaration.

The use of defaults can avoid the use of the normal suffixes (!,#,%,&,$) but at the expense of making a reader of the program listing continually need to refer back to find what type is being used. It is particularly irritating if several variables over-ride the defaults.

DIM

Type:	Statement.
Typical syntax:	DIM arrayname(number)
	DIM arrayname(lower TO upper)
	DIM variable AS type
Action:	Declares an array variable and the size of the array, or specifies the type of a scalar (non-array) variable.
Options:	DIM can be followed by SHARED to indicate that a variable will be global to all parts of the program
Argument(s):	The maximum number of items in the array, or the range of possible item numbers, enclosed in brackets.
Restrictions:	The lowest possible subscript will be 0 unless OPTION BASE 1 has been used or the DIM statement specifies some lower limit.

Examples:

(a)
```
DIM A$(100)
REM Permits array A$ to hold a maximum of 101 strings.
REM subscripts 0 to 100
```

(b)
```
DIM Intarray (10 TO 100)
REM Allows Values of Intarray(10) to Intarray(100)
REM to be used.
```

(c)
```
DIM Article AS STRING * 20
REM allows Article to be used as a string variable
REM of fixed size, 20 characters.
```

(d)
```
DIM Nomen AS STRING, num AS INT, nim AS DOUBLE
REM several in one DIM line
Nomen = "Ian Sinclair"        'assign string
num = 226                      'assign integer
nim = 1326557.839             'assign double
```

(e)
```
DIM SHARED examp AS STRING
REM string examp can be used by all SUB procedures
REM and all functions in the program.
```

Associated with: COMMON, $DYNAMIC, ERASE, OPTION BASE, REDIM, SHARED, $STATIC

Points to note:

DIM used with a number, such as DIM A$(100) creates a static array, prepared before the program runs. DIM used with a number variable, such as DIM A$(N%) creates a dynamic array, prepared when the program runs. These defaults can be over-ridden by specifying that arrays are static or dynamic. See Appendix B for the meaning of static and dynamic arrays.

You cannot use a list of names followed by the AS statement. For example, a line such as:

```
DIM Able, Baker, Charlie AS STRING
```

is not valid – none of these will be taken as a string variable and you will see a Type Mismatch message when you try to run the program.

Note the use of SHARED following DIM for a global variable name. SHARED can also be used for more restricted sharing.

DO

Type:	Statement.	
Typical syntax:	DO UNTIL condition	DO WHILE condition
	Statements	Statements
	LOOP	LOOP
	DO	DO
	Statements	Statements
	LOOP UNTIL condition	LOOP WHILE condition.
Action:	Creates a loop that runs until a condition is true (or while it is untrue) or while a condition is true (or until it is untrue). The loop can be tested at either end.	
Options:	Can be used with UNTIL or WHILE conditions, with condition testing at start or at end of the loop. Another option is to use no conditions with DO or LOOP and terminate the loop by using an EXIT line, see entry for EXIT.	
Argument(s):	None	
Restrictions:	If the loop is tested at the start, the variable that is tested may need to be assigned a dummy value.	

Examples:

(a)
```
DO UNTIL Entry% => 100    'start, tested variable = 0
   INPUT Entry%           'item entered
LOOP                      'item will be tested
```

(b)
```
DO                        'start, no test
   INPUT Entry%           'item input
WHILE Entry% < 101        'test here of entered item
```

(c)
```
Entry$ = "dummy"          'dummy value needed
DO WHILE Entry$ <>""      'to make test TRUE
   INPUT Entry$           'input real value
LOOP                      'loop back to test
```

(d)
```
Entry$ = "dummy"          'dummy value needed
DO UNTIL Entry$ = ""      'to make test TRUE
   INPUT Entry$           'input real value
LOOP                      'loop back to test
```

Associated with: EXIT, FOR, NEXT, LOOP, WHILE, WEND

Points to note:

If the LOOP UNTIL or LOOP WHILE form is used, the loop will run at least once, because the condition cannot be tested until the end of the loop. This may require a variable that is tested to be assigned a dummy value before the loop starts. If the DO UNTIL or DO WHILE form is used, the condition is tested before the loop starts and if the condition is unsuitable the loop will not run. The options of UNTIL and WHILE avoid the need for using clauses such as NOT A < B that include an inversion of the logic.

The DO...LOOP form should be used in place of older forms such as WHILE...WEND because it can be constructed in four ways, as the examples show. If testing at the start and the end is not sufficient, the EXIT statements can be used to allow the loop to be terminated by a test made inside the loop. For example:

```
CLS
DO
READ a$
IF a$ = "X" THEN EXIT DO
PRINT a$
LOOP
DATA Glenfiddich, Glenmorangie, Laphroaig
DATA Islay Mist, Talisker, X
```

has no test at either the DO end or the LOOP end, only in the middle. This allows a quantity that will stop the loop to be read and the loop stopped before this quantity is processed. Using EXIT avoids the problems that sometimes cause printing a blank item or printing a terminator item.

DRAW

Type: Statement.

Typical syntax: DRAW command$

Action: Draws a geometrical shape from the list of commands provided in string form as an argument.

Options:
D Moves cursor down.
E Moves cursor up and right.
F Moves cursor down and right.
G Moves cursor down and left.
H Moves cursor up and left.
L Moves cursor left.
R Moves cursor right.
U Moves cursor up.

Each of these letters is followed by an integer number to determine the amount of movement. If no number is provided, the movement is one screen pixel in the direction stated.

M   Moves cursor to point x%,y%

M+ Moves cursor to position, adding co-ordinates to current

M- Moves cursor to position, subtracting co-ordinates from current

Each of these letter commands is followed by a pair of co-ordinate numbers separated by a comma. There are two option letters that can be used ahead of M, M+ or M :

B   Option to move cursor without drawing.

N   Option to draw and return cursor to its original position.

A   Rotates an object anticlockwise by units of 90 degrees.

Followed by 0, 1, 2 or 3 for number of 90° anticlockwise steps.

C   Sets the drawing colour.

P   Sets the paint fill and border colours of an object

C is followed by a single colour number, P is followed by one number for fill and one for border.

S sets the scale of the drawing by using an integer. The default is 4 for a scale of 1 pixel unit (causing no change in drawing scale). Numbers lower than 4 cause a reduced scale, larger numbers cause an enlarged scale.

TA turns a shape by a specified number of degrees of angle. Number range is +360 to -360, with a positive number turning anticlockwise, negative clockwise. A number exceeding 360 causes an error.

X calls a draw subroutine.

The X command must be followed by a pointer to the address of the drawing string that is used as a subroutine, using VARPTR$.

Argument(s): A string of option letters. The string can be formed in advance by assignment, allowing you to use DRAW D$, or the letters can be used directly within quotes.

Restrictions: Variable names cannot be used directly for numbers, only by way of VARPTR$. For example, you cannot use "UK%", where K% represents a number of steps for the up command, but you can use "U" + VARPTR$(K%)

The size of a unit movement is equal in both X and Y directions only for the VGA screen in 640 x 480 modes. For other graphics screens, sizes must be adjusted to allow for the pixels being rectangular. Low resolution screens can have X to Y distance ratios of 5:6 or 5:12, making the use of DRAW instruction less easy. Fortunately, modern computers have standardised the use of VGA screens.

Examples:

(a)   `DRAW "MB100,100C12U20R20D20L20"`

        `REM Draws a box starting at 100,100`

(b)   `DRAW A$ + "X" + VARPTR$(B$)`

        `REM Draws using commands in A$ and adds commands in B$`

Associated with: PALETTE, PALETTE USING, SCREEN, VARPTR$

Points to note:

VARPTR$ is a function that is intended for use with DRAW and PLAY only. DRAW is a form of macro statement which allows elaborate drawings to be made with great ease, because the drawings can be designed on squared paper and the squares counted to find the correct numbers to use with the DRAW commands. The use of the X command for a draw subroutine allows small repetitive detail to be added with very little effort.

The use of the S scaling factor means that if a drawing routine has been made in the wrong size it can be altered without the need to alter each number in the string.

To avoid typing DRAW strings which are too wide to be printed, assign your DRAW strings in portions and add them into one variable before using DRAW, or use + signs in the DRAW argument. For example, you can use:

```
A$ = "........(set of options).........."
B$ = "........(set of options).........."
C$ = "........(set of options).........."
```

and then either:

```
D$ = A$ + B$ + C$
DRAW D$
```

or

```
DRAW A$ + B$ + C$
```

This is a practical point which is not mentioned in manuals.

$DYNAMIC

Type:	Metacommand
Typical syntax:	REM $DYNAMIC or ' $DYNAMIC
Action:	Ensures that arrays declared in any following DIM statements are by default dynamic (see Appendix B).
Options:	None.
Argument(s):	None.
Restrictions:	The array type can be over-ridden in a subsequent DIM statement if required.

Example:

```
REM $DYNAMIC
DIM A$(20), B$(20,5)
REM will make arrays A$ and B$ dynamic rather than static.
```

Associated with: DIM, REDIM, REM, SHARED, STATIC

Points to note:

Used mainly for compatibility with compiled BASIC programs. It is easier to use the DIM statement itself to allocate the array type. The default static array is usually the better choice because it allows faster array use (because the array is permanently set up in memory rather than being created as required).

ELSE

Type:	Statement.
Typical syntax:	ELSE action
Action:	Carries out a statement or set of statements when preceding IF tests have failed.
Options:	Can be followed by a another test using IF
Argument(s):	None.
Restrictions:	Can be used only as part of an IF...THEN set of tests.

Example:

```
IF K% = 5 GOSUB Fiveone         'run this for 5
   ELSE IF k% = 2 GOSUB Twoone 'run this for 2
   ELSE GOSUB Otherone          'run this for any other
END IF
```

Associated with: CASE IF, ON GOSUB, ON GOTO, THEN

Points to note:

A SELECT CASE structure is usually easier to construct and to understand than a set of ELSE IF clauses. When a set of ELSE IF statements forms part of an elaborate IF...END IF set of tests, it can often be very difficult to understand exactly what is happening. Using SELECT...CASE usually results in much clearer statements.

END

Type:	Statement.
Typical syntax:	END
	END DEF
	END FUNCTION
	END IF
	END SELECT
	END SUB
	END TYPE

Action: Marks the end of a program, or the end of a block of lines used in a definition, see Arguments.

Options: None

Argument(s):

DEF	to end a DEF FN of several lines.
FUNCTION	to end a FUNCTION procedure definition.
IF	to end an IF...THEN...ELSE statement of several lines.
SELECT	to end a SELECT CASE set of lines.
SUB	to end a SUB procedure definition.
TYPE	to end a user-defined data type (record) definition.

Restrictions: END used alone will terminate a program at that point. All open files will be closed, and control will return to the QBASIC editor.

Example:

```
PRINT "End of Program"
END
Firstsub: D%=15
. . . . . . . . . . .
RETURN
```

Associated with: DEF FN, FUNCTION, IF, THEN, ELSE, SELECT CASE, STOP, SUB, SYSTEM, TYPE

Points to note:

The END statement, with no argument, must be used ahead of any subroutines of the GOSUB type to prevent the subroutines from being run unintentionally (crashing through). A program can contain more than one END statement, usually to prevent sections being run unintentionally. This is less of a problem when the modern procedures (SUB) and functions of

QBASIC are used, because these are *transparent* in the sense that they are executed only when called – the interpreter skips over them unless they have been called.

When a statement uses several lines of statements in a block, an END along with the type name is needed to mark the end of the block. Failure to include this will cause an error whose type will depend on what piece of program has been accidentally run (such as a READ, causing an Out of Data).

ENVIRON

Type:	Statement.
Typical syntax:	ENVIRON string
Action:	Allows the value of an environment variable (see Appendix D) to be changed to a new value set by a string used as the argument. Also allows a new environment variable to be created and used.
Options:	None.
Argument(s):	A string consisting of name and setting for environment variable.
Restrictions:	Some environment variables should not be changed, such as the COMSPEC environment. If the COMSPEC value is changed, the computer may not be able to find the essential portion of MS-DOS. See Notes for how to change the environment space.
Example:	

```
ENVIRON ("PATH = C:\;
C:\MSDOS;C:\QBASIC")
REM Establishes this search path for file
REM while you are using QBASIC
```

Associated with: ENVIRON$ function, PATH, PROMPT

Points to note:

You do not need to cancel the effects of ENVIRON (unless your program requires this) because the original values are restored when the program ends. This avoids the drastic effects on MS-DOS actions that could result if you quit QBASIC with all of the environment variables changed.

To delete an environment value, place only a semicolon following the equals sign. For example:

```
ENVIRON "PATH=;"
```

will remove all assignments to the PATH environment variable.

The environment space (the memory assigned for environment variables) cannot be changed in QBASIC. The default value, set in MS-DOS, is 256 bytes. To change the environment space, edit the CONFIG.SYS in the root directory of your computer, altering the SHELL statement.

The SHELL statement is used in CONFIG.SYS as a way of indicating where the main MS-DOS command file is located, and whether it is permanent or not. It can also be used to alter the default environment size by adding a section such as /E:1024. For example, if the SHELL line in your CONFIG.SYS line looks like this:

SHELL = C:\MSDOS\COMMAND.COM C:\MSDOS\ /P

you can increase the environment to 1024 bytes by adding /E:1024 to make the line appear as:

SHELL = C:\MSDOS\COMMAND.COM C:\MSDOS\ /E:1024 /P

You should not, on any account, alter any existing part of the line.

ENVIRON$

Type:	Function returning string
Typical syntax:	PRINT ENVIRON$ ("PATH") PRINT ENVIRON$ (2)
Action:	Returns the value of an environment string set up in DOS, such as PATH or PROMPT.
Options:	None.
Argument(s):	A string consisting of the name of an environment variable (see Appendix D), or an integer number to indicate the position of an environment variable in a list. The argument must be enclosed in brackets.
Restrictions:	The environment variables must have been created by DOS or by the QBASIC program (see ENVIRON) before the function can be valid.

Examples:

(a)
```
ENV$ = ENVIRON$("PROMPT")
REM ENV$ will carry PROMPT assignment
```

(b)
```
PRINT ENVIRON$ (2)
REM Prints second environment string
```

Associated with: ENVIRON Statement, PATH, PROMPT

Points to note:

Can be used along with the ENVIRON statement to extend a path or change a prompt temporarily.

EOF

Type:	Function returning Boolean (TRUE or FALSE)
Typical syntax:	IF EOF(filenumber)
Action:	Returns TRUE at the end of a sequential file, FALSE if there are remaining records in the file.
Options:	None.
Argument(s):	The file number as established by the OPEN statement, without the hash sign, and enclosed in brackets.
Restrictions:	The EOF() test should be put at the end of a loop used to read the file, because EOF occurs *after* the last file has been read. This is an important point if you are converting programs from the older BASICA or GW BASIC. In these versions, the test for EOF could be made at the start of a WHILE…WEND loop, but this cannot be done in QBASIC.

Example:

```
DEFINT A-Z
CLS
OPEN "aircraft.dat" FOR INPUT AS #6 'open file for reading
PRINT TAB(27); "DATA DISPLAY"
PRINT
DO
  INPUT #6, name$                    'get first record
  PRINT "Name of this record- "; name$     'use first item
  RESTORE                            'data list at start
  PRINT
  FOR n = 1 TO 5                     'start reading data items
    READ head$                       'to use as headings
    INPUT #6, gen$                   'get data from file
    PRINT head$; " - "; gen$         'print both
  NEXT
  PRINT
  PRINT "Press any key for next record"
  k$ = INPUT$(1)                     'get key
LOOP UNTIL EOF(6)                    'repeat until end of file
```

```
CLOSE                                    'close file
PRINT "End of file"
END
DATA country of origin,type,power,empty weight,accommodation
```

Associated with: OPEN, INPUT #, PRINT #, WRITE #

Points to note:

EOF is valid only for sequential data files and for items read through the serial communications port (when it indicates that the buffer is empty). EOF has no meaning for a random-access file.

ERDEV

Type:	Function
Typical syntax:	ERDEV
Action:	Returns a code for error number and the device that caused the error. The low byte of this integer is the error code, the high byte is the device or attribute code. These numbers can be found as indicated in Notes below.
Options:	None
Argument(s):	None
Restrictions:	Used in error handling subroutines only, and intended for use in ON ERROR GOTO routines.

Example:

```
ON ERROR GOTO report
A$ = "NAME"
LPRINT A$          'keep printer switched off
END
report:
PRINT "Device error number is "; ERDEV
```

Associated with: ERDEV$, ERL, ERR, ERROR, ON ERROR, RESUME

Points to note:

The error codes are critical error codes such as Drive not ready, Printer out of paper etc. In a few cases, the ERDEV number includes further information on device attributes, and when this happens the codes are found as follows:

The device attributes code is INT(ERDEV/256), the integer part of the ERDEV number divided by 256. This is the high byte of the 2-byte integer number. For many devices this will be zero, so that using ERDEV provides the error code completely.

The error code is ERDEV MOD 256, which is the low byte of the ERDEV integer number.

The error numbers for devices are not the error numbers listed in Appendix E. A printer not ready error, for example, is 10, and a CHDIR "A:\" (with no disk in the A: drive) is error 2. The device names that ERDEV$ returns are also not as you might expect for some items.

Some device errors may cause unexpected results by not altering ERDEV or ERDEV$. This allows these variables to retain the values they obtained for the previous error, causing confusion. The following example will print the same disk error three times because ERDEV is not being changed by the COM3 lines:

```
CLS
ON ERROR GOTO fixit
A$ = "Nothing"
LPRINT A$        'printer off, first error
CHDIR "A:\"      'no disk in drive, second error
OPEN "COM3:" FOR INPUT AS #1      'no COM3
INPUT #1, a$                      'no input
END
fixit:
PRINT ERDEV, ERDEV$              'print results
RESUME NEXT                      'next error
```

This routine prints 10 M: for the printer error and 2 A: for the disk error, and then repeats the 2 A: report two more times.

Note that any error which returns an ERDEV number will return an ERR number also, see entry for ERR. This ERR number will not be the same as the ERDEV number.

ERDEV$

Type:	Function
Typical syntax:	PRINT ERDEV$
Action:	Carries the code-name of device causing an error, such as M: for printer, A:, B: or C: (block devices).
Options:	None.
Argument(s):	None.
Restrictions:	Used in error-handling routines only

Example:

```
ON ERROR GOTO geterr
REM Keep printer switched off
LPRINT "TEST"
END
geterr:
PRINT "Error in "; ERDEV$
REM Should indicate error
END
```

Associated with: ERDEV, ERL, ERR, ERROR, ON ERROR, RESUME

Points to note:

Returns the abbreviated name of the device rather than a code. Can cause confusion if the error string has not changed since the previous error, see ERDEV entry.

ERL

Type:	Function returning integer number.
Typical syntax:	PRINT ERL
Action:	Carries an integer number which is the line number for the line causing an error.
Options:	None.
Argument(s):	None.
Restrictions:	Intended to be used only in error-handling routines and only for older programs which use line numbers. Where lines are labelled ERL can return only the last-used number, and if no lines are numbered ERL will return zero. This makes ERL unsuitable for use in modern QBASIC programs.

Example:

```
PRINT "Error occurred in line "; ERL
```

Associated with: ERDEV, ERDEV$, ERR, ERROR, RESUME

Points to note:

Should not be used in any new program, retained only for compatibility. Error tracing in QBASIC is done mainly by way of the Editor, and where a program contains error-trapping the use of ERL is redundant.

ERR

Type:	Function returning integer number.
Typical syntax:	PRINT ERR
	IF ERR = number THEN
Action:	Returns the error code for the most recent error that was trapped. See Appendix E for a list of run-time error codes.
Options:	None.
Argument(s):	None.
Restrictions:	Intended to be used only in error-trapping routines that are activated by using an ON ERROR GOTO line.

Example:

```
CLS
ON ERROR GOTO fixit
FOR J% = 1 TO 3
 READ A$
NEXT
PRINT A$
END
DATA Jones, Green
fixit:
PRINT "Error type "; ERR: "occurred"
IF ERR = 4 THEN RESTORE    'Restores DATA list when out of data
RESUME                     'try again
REM Prints Jones
```

Associated with: ERDEV, ERDEV$, ERL, ERROR, ON ERROR GOTO, RESUME, RESUME NEXT

Points to note:

See Error number list, Appendix E.

ERROR

Type:	Statement
Typical syntax:	ERROR number
Action:	Used to create an error artificially, allowing the response of a program to the error to be tested. Normally used to test ON ERROR GOTO routines.
Options:	None.
Argument(s):	Number of error to be simulated
Restrictions:	Error codes can use numbers 0 to 255, but the error codes for QBASIC extend only to 76, see Appendix E. Error numbers greater than 76 are user-defined.

Example:

```
CLS
ON ERROR GOTO sortit          'error routine
FOR n% = 1 TO 10              ' only 6 possible
   READ j%
   PRINT j%
endloop:
NEXT
backhere:
PRINT "The next message has been forced by the ERROR
command"
ON ERROR GOTO 0               'disables error handling
ERROR 61                      'Disk full error triggered
END                          ' to show effect
DATA 1,2,3,4,5,6,

sortit:                       'error routine
IF ERR = 4 THEN RESUME endloop 'out of data error
RESUME backhere               'following loop
REM Normally this routine would be extended to deal
REM with the Disk Full error also if it is likely
REM to arise. Using ERROR 61 allows the response to
REM such an error to be tested without the
REM inconvenience of filling a disk.
```

Associated with: ERDEV, ERDEV$, ERL, ERR, RESUME

Points to note:

Other error codes can be used if an ON ERROR GOTO leads to an error-handler for the numbers. You can, for example use:

ERROR 100

at some point in a program and in the error-trapping routine place a line such as:

IF ERROR = 100 THEN

    (Statements)

END IF

to deal with this *error.* This use of a user-defined error is not exactly common, but it can be used for testing purposes.

EXIT

Type:	Statement

Typical syntax: EXIT DEF   EXIT DO   EXIT FOR
                      EXIT FUNCTION   EXIT SUB

Action: Breaks out of a block of statements that are part of a
                      structure such as DEF, DO, FOR, FUNCTION or SUB

Options: None.

Argument(s):   Name of structure as shown above.

Restrictions: Normally used as the result of a test in the middle of a
                      loop. There is no EXIT provision for the obsolescent
                      WHILE…WEND loop.

Example:

```
CLS
DO                              'loop with no condition
READ a$                        'action
IF a$ = "END" THEN EXIT DO     'escape clause
PRINT a$                       'will not print END
LOOP                           'end of loop
DATA AJS, BSA, Calthorpe, Enfield, Francis-Barnett
DATA Harley-Davidson, Indian, J.A.P., Matchless, END
```

Associated with: DEF FN, DO...LOOP, FOR...NEXT, FUNCTION, SUB

Points to note:

EXIT cannot be used alone; it must have an argument which is one of
these listed. When EXIT is used it will *tidy up* the loop that it has left, so
that nothing remains (on the stack) from the loop. Other methods of
leaving a loop (notoriously by using a GOTO) can leave addresses on the
stack, causing problems if this is done too often in a program run. Using
EXIT avoids the need for actions such as setting the end condition
artificially, and ensures that the loop is ended at the point where the EXIT
statement is used.

EXP

Type:	Function returning number
Typical syntax:	K = EXP(number)
Action:	Returns the number which is ex where x is the argument and e is the exponential function (see Notes).
Options:	None.
Argument(s):	A number or number variable which is to be the power of e, enclosed in brackets.
Restrictions:	Do not use numbers greater than 88.02969 as an argument.

Example:

```
CLS
X = .59
PRINT "Sinh(X) is "; (EXP(X) - EXP(-X))/2
PRINT "2 to the power 10 is" INT(EXP(LOG(2) * 10))
```

Associated with: LOG

Points to note:

If $A = LOG(K)$ then $K = EXP(A)$, so that EXP performs an antilog action for LOG.

The exponential function is a natural function which occurs whenever a rate of change is affected by a remaining amount. For example, when water drips from a leaky container, its rate of flow is fast when there is a lot of water in the container, but slower when the amount of water decreases. The discharge of a capacitor, decay of radiation and other natural processes follow the same form of law, using an equation of the form:

$$X = X_0 e^{-at}$$

where X is the amount remaining after a time t seconds, X_0 is the original quantity and a is the factor that controls the rate (such as the size of the leak in the water-can).

Rather confusingly, any function of the form:

$$y = a^x$$

is described by mathematicians as exponential, and this is also the meaning implied in terms like exponential growth (or an investment, for example) or exponential decay. The EXP function is concerned only when the factor whose power is taken is the natural constante.

FIELD

Type:	Statement
Typical syntax:	FIELD filenumber size AS fieldname, size AS fieldname…
Action:	Prepares for random-access file use by allocating space for variables. Old type of statement, see Notes.
Options:	None.
Argument(s):	The number (handle) of an open file (see OPEN statement), followed by field size and name definitions.
Restrictions:	The filename that is used must not be re-assigned.

Example:

```
FILE% = 1                  'file number to use
LIMIT% = 100               'loop limit
OPEN "integer.rnd" FOR RANDOM AS #FILE% LEN = 2 'open file
FIELD FILE%, 2 AS A$       'two byte records
FOR N% = 1 TO LIMIT%       'start loop
A% = 1000 - N%             'generate recognisable number!
LSET A$ = MKI$(A%)         'set in field
PUT FILE%                  'put in file
NEXT                       'loop back
CLOSE                      'close file
REM opens random access file for a file of integers
REM and records a set.
```

Associated with: GET, LSET, PUT, RSET, TYPE

Points to note:

This statement should be used for compatibility only. For new programs, create a user-defined variable type rather than using the clumsy FIELD expressions.

All fields in a random-access file are of strings, so that the names used in the FIELD statement are all string names, either using the dollar suffix or declared as string names by using DEFSTR or by DIM statements.

FILEATTR

Type:	Function
Typical syntax:	FILEATTR (filenumber, attribute number)
Action:	For an open file, returns either the file handle number or a number that indicates the type of OPEN statement.
Options:	None.
Argument(s):	The number of an open file, and the attribute whose value is to be returned. When the attribute number is 2, FILEATTR returns the DOS file handle number. When the attribute number is 1, the function will return:

2	for	Output
4	for	Random
8	for	Append
32	for	Binary

The arguments should be seperated by a comma and enclosed in brackets.

Restrictions: The file must be open.

Example:

```
OPEN "MYFILE.SER" FOR APPEND AS #2    'open file
PRINT FILEATTR(2,1)                   'prints 8
CLOSE #2                              'close file
```

Associated with: OPEN, CLOSE

Points to note:

The use of attribute number 2 is seldom, if ever, needed. It is unusual to need FILEATTR at all because when an OPEN statement has been used in a program, you usually know what type of file has been opened because this has been specified in the OPEN statement. FILEATTR is used when a range of file handle numbers is being used, and due to the order in which subroutines have run there would be no way of knowing which OPEN statement had assigned a given file number.

FILES

Type:	Statement
Typical syntax:	FILES "drive:\path"
Action:	Produces a directory of files in a specified drive or directory.
Options:	None.
Argument(s):	The drive, or drive and path to files, expressed as a string.
Restrictions:	An error will be signalled if the drive or directory does not exist, or if the arguments are not in string form.

Example:
```
CLS
current$ = "C:\"      'directory that contains QBASIC
parent$ = ".."        'next directory closer to root
floppy$ = "A:"        'floppy drive
FILES (current$)      'print current directory
FILES (parent$)       'print parent directory
FILES (floppy$)       'print directory of A
END
```

Associated with: CHDIR, MKDIR, RMDIR

Points to note:

FILES is used to display any directory, and is the QBASIC equivalent of the MS-DOS DIR command. FILES can be used with the wildcard characters ? and * . For example, a line such as:

FILES ("*.BAS")

will list only the files in the current directory which have the BAS extension and the line:

FILES ("TE?T.DOC)

will find files named, for example, TEXT.DOC, TEST.DOC, TENT.DOC, TEUT.DOC and so on. The asterisk can take the place of any set of characters; the question-mark can take the place of any single character. These wildcards are used exactly as they are in the MS-DOS DIR command.

FIX

Type:	Function returning integer or long integer
Typical syntax:	number variable = FIX(number)
Action:	Removes any fractional part of a number to return an integer or long integer number. There is *no* rounding action.
Options:	None.
Argument(s):	The number, number variable, or expression to be sliced to an integer (truncated), held within brackets.
Restrictions:	The Number must be capable of being expressed as an integer or long integer when a fraction is stripped, so that the range of numbers is restricted to the range of a long integer, from -2,147,483,648 to +2,147,483,647.

Example:

```
FOR N% = 1 TO 2
  READ A, B#
  PRINT A; " reduces to "; FIX(A)
  PRINT B#; " reduces to "; FIX(B#)
NEXT
DATA 1.56, 23157.05698, 27.66, 1015007.57294
```

Associated with: CINT, CLNG, FIX, INT

Points to note:

Use INT for rounding actions, FIX to strip off a fraction. An alternative for numbers in the integer or long integer range is to assign the number to a variable of integer or long integer type.

FOR

Type: Statement

Typical syntax: FOR start number TO end number
　　Statements
　NEXT

Action: Starts a loop that depends on the incrementing and testing of a number variable. The loop end is marked by the NEXT statement.

Options: The STEP number clause, placed following the end number of FOR, will determine the interval to be used.

The NEXT statement can use the counter variable as an argument in the form:

NEXT j%

but an error will result if this variable name does not match the one used in the FOR part of the statement.

Argument(s): The start number followed by the TO clause and the optional STEP clause.

Restrictions: Used with number counts only. FOR without NEXT and NEXT without FOR are errors. Each FOR must have a matching NEXT. The loop will not run if the values are impossible, such as:

FOR x% = 10 TO 1

or

FOR X% = 1 TO 10 STEP -1

Examples:

(a)
```
FOR n% = 1 TO 100 STEP 10    'loop conditions, step 10
PRINT "Value is "; n%        'look at values
NEXT
```

(b)
```
CLS
FOR n% = 1 TO 10             'outer loop
  PRINT "Count is"; n%       'prints number
  FOR j = 1 TO 1200: NEXT    'inner (nested) timing loop
  CLS                        'clear
NEXT                         'back to start of outer loop
```

(c)
```
FOR n = 1 TO 5 STEP .01        'float variable, small step
   PRINT "Fractional"; n        'look at these numbers
NEXT
REM shows cumulative effects of imprecision of a
REM single-precision variable.
```

(d)
```
CLS
FOR n% = 1 TO 1000                              'large loop
   INPUT "name, please (type X to end) "; name$ 'input name
   IF UCASE$(name$) = "X" THEN EXIT FOR          'other exit
NEXT                                            'normal loop
PRINT "End of entries"
REM demonstrates jumping out of loop other than
REM by ending the count
```

Associated with: DO, EXIT, LOOP, WHILE, WEND

Points to note:

Use an EXIT FOR statement to provide a premature end to the loop, for example by providing a terminator number. *Never* jump out of a FOR...NEXT loop by using a GOTO statement because this can produce corruption in the stack. The use of EXIT FOR provides for an orderly end of the loop even if the count has not terminated normally. This also allows the loop to be ended by more than one condition and in more than one place in the loop.

Where a set of loops is nested, a single NEXT can be used if all of the loops terminate in the same line. Such a single NEXT must use the variables for all the loops in the form:

```
NEXT k%,J%,i%
```

- using the variables in the correct order of termination of loops, which is the opposite of the order of opening loops. Incorrect nesting order will lead to an error message, usually a NEXT without FOR.

When the loop counter variable is a floating-point number and the STEP number is also a floating-point number, the use of Single precision can result in a loss of precision which is cumulative, as example (c) shows. A loop using float variables runs much less quickly than one using integers, so that integer variables should be used if at all possible.

The use of a FOR...NEXT loop as a time delay is not necessary in QBASIC because the SLEEP statement can produce a delay whose timing is the same for whatever machine is being used.

Use DO loops where no counting action is involved.

FRE

Type:	Function returning integer number
Typical syntax:	FRE(number) or FRE(string)
Action:	Returns the amount of memory available for use in a specified way.
Options:	None
Argument(s):	A number, number variable, string or string variable, enclosed in brackets. The string can be a dummy.
	Using an argument of -1 causes FRE to return the size of the largest number array that can be used.
	With an argument of -2, the unused stack space is returned.
	With any other number, the available string space is returned.
	When a string argument is used, any unused string space (due to deleted strings) is collected, and the total amount of string space is returned.
Restrictions:	Number values -1 or -2 have special effects. Only the free amount in one segment (see Appendix C) is returned.
Example:	

```
PRINT FRE(-1)
PRINT FRE(-2)
PRINT FRE("")
```

Associated with: CLEAR (to change stack size)

Points to note:

Stack space can be important for a program using recursion, because each recursive step will place some code on the stack. This can limit the number of recursions, typically to seven.

FREEFILE

Type:	Function returning integer
Typical syntax:	intvariable = FREEFILE
Action:	Returns the next available file number that can be used for any type of file OPEN statement.
Options:	None.
Argument(s):	None.
Restrictions:	A file must already be open
Example:	

```
OPEN "SERFILE" FOR APPEND AS f%
k% = FREEFILE
OPEN "NEWFILE" FOR OUTPUT AS k%
```

Associated with: GET, OPEN, PUT

Points to note:

This is useful mainly when a program can use various file-handling subroutines in an order that depends on menu choices. Using FREEFILE, the program allocates file handle numbers for itself, rather than depending on fixed numbers allocated by the programmer. This is not for the faint-hearted, because it can be very difficult to find during debugging which subroutine opened a file. It is better to use a fixed file handle number wherever possible.

FUNCTION

Type: Statement

Typical syntax: FUNCTION name (parameters)
                         statements
                         name = expression
                        END FUNCTION

Action: Defines the name, data type, and action for a FUNCTION procedure.

Options: STATIC can be used following parameters to ensure that the values of local variables are preserved between calls to the FUNCTION.

Argument(s):   Function name and (optional) parameter list. Any parameters used must be enclosed in brackets.

Restrictions: The name must include a data type suffix, such as Nomen#, Nombre$ etc. There is no form of declaration that can be used for the function type. Parameters can be specified as A, B$, C# or in the form:

able AS DOUBLE,

baker AS STRING

and so on. The return value is supplied by using the line:

name = expression.

Example:

(a)
```
FUNCTION sumofsq (x,y)          'header line
sumofsq = SQR(x ^ 2 + y ^ 2)    'defines number returned
END FUNCTION                    'end of block
```

(b)
```
DECLARE FUNCTION geteqn! (a!, b!, c!) 'declares function
CLS
a = 2.5                         'quantities to
b = 5.4                         'function
c = 2.2                         'function
y = geteqn(a, b, c)             'call the function
PRINT "Y is"; y                 'print result
END
```

```
FUNCTION geteqn (a, b, c)        'definition of function
geteqn = a ^ 2 + 6 * b + c       'assign returned number
END FUNCTION                     'end marker
```

Associated with: DECLARE, DEF FN, EXIT, SHARED, STATIC, SUB

Points to note:

This is the modern replacement for the DEF FN statement. When the function is called, using brackets for arguments will ensure that these values are not changed. As a demonstration:

```
DECLARE FUNCTION testfunc! (x!, y!)
CLS
a = 2                         'assign
b = 3                         'values
PRINT testfunc((a), b)        'variable a in brackets
PRINT a, b                    'a is 2, b is 33
END

FUNCTION testfunc (x, y)
x = 22                        'assignments
y = 33
testfunc = x                  'dummy, not used
END FUNCTION
```

shows that the value of **b** has been changed by the assignment in the function, but the value of **a** has not changed because of the brackets. This makes the use of parameters in a Function more flexible. The older DEF FN type of function was much more restricted in passing back values.

GET (File)

Type:	Statement
Typical syntax:	GET filenumber
	GET filenumber, recordnumber
	GET filenumber, recordnumber, variablename
Action:	Reads a byte or data unit from a random-access file and can assign a variable.
Options:	For random access and binary files a record (or byte) number can be used to locate a position in the file. A variable name can also be used to provide a variable to which the filed data can be assigned.
Argument(s):	The number of an open file, optional record position number and variable to assign to.
Restrictions:	The maximum record or byte number is 16,777,215. The variable must be a string variable or a user-defined variable type.

Example:

```
OPEN "RANFIL.RND" FOR RANDOM AS #1
GET #1, 1, item$        'assign record to item$
PRINT item$             'print it
CLOSE
REM Normally item$ would consist of a set of strings
REM which would be split up either by using their
REM names as in the FIELD statement, or by using the names
REM assigned in a user-defined type, see TYPE
```

Associated with: FIELD, Graphics GET and PUT, LOCATE, LSET, RSET, MKD$, MKI$, MKL$, MKS$, CVD, CVI, CVL, CVS, TYPE

Points to note:

The # in the file-number is optional, but useful as a way of distinguishing the handle number. The record position number will read the specified record of a random file or the specified byte in a binary file.

Older versions of BASIC may use GET without the option to include a variable name as an argument.

If no record / byte number is used, the GET statement will read the next record or byte in sequence, starting at the first if the file has not been read or any LOC function used.

If you specify a variable name but not a record number, the two commas must not be omitted.

GET (Graphics)

Type:	Statement
Typical syntax:	GET picture-range, arrayname
Action:	Stores a screen pattern in the form of an array which can be saved if required.
Options:	Using STEP ahead of the co-ordinate numbers allows co-ordinates to be taken as relative to the existing cursor position.
Argument(s):	The picture range consists of the co-ordinates of the upper left-hand corner of the picture followed by the lower right-hand corner, separated by a hyphen. The arrayname defines the array which will be used to store the picture. The starting number for the array can be specified.
Restrictions:	The co-ordinate number pairs must be bracketed and separated by a hyphen, numbers separated by a comma. The array must be adequately dimensioned, see notes.

Examples:

(a)
```
GET (x%,y%) - (a%,b%), Pix% 'The array is Pix%
```

(b)
```
DIM pix%(255)
SCREEN 1                 'low resolution
CIRCLE (15, 15), 9,1 'draw circle
GET (0, 0) - (30, 30), Pix% 'get into array
FOR j% = 1 TO 5         'start loop
   PUT (j% * 32, 80), Pix%   'put images back
NEXT                     'at different places
END
REM Error if PUT co-ordinates are outside screen
REM area for selected SCREEN number.
```

Associated with: PUT, SCREEN

Points to note:

Using an array value such as Pix%(10) will make this the first value to hold the GET data.

The main difficulty in using GET is calculating the size of the array that is needed. This should be an integer array, which stores two bytes per integer. The formula for the dimension of the array is:

(4 + INT((X * bits) + 7) / 8) * Y) / 2

and the bits factor is the number of binary bits that are needed to store each pixel. This depends on the screen type as follows:

Screen Mode	Bits per pixel
1	2
2	1
7	4
8	4
9	4
10	2
11	1
12	4
13	8

For example, using SCREEN 12 and storing an array that is 200 pixels wide by 50 pixels high, the array dimension that is needed is:

(4 + INT((200 * 4 + 7) / 8) * 50) / 2

which is 2502 integer numbers. If the array is to be Pix%, it will be dimensioned by the line:

DIM Pix%(2502)

This array can be saved as a sequential or binary file so that screen patterns can be stored on disk and retrieved subsequently to be replaced with PUT. This technique is easier to use with high-resolution screens than BLOAD and BSAVE

GOSUB

Type:	Statement
Typical syntax:	GOSUB linereference
Action:	Branches to a subroutine. The RETURN statement in the subroutine will cause the return, optionally to a nominated line.
Options:	None.
Argument(s):	A line number or a line label name.
Restrictions:	The subroutine must be placed following the END of the program to prevent accidental entry (crashing through). Using GOSUB without RETURN, or RETURN without GOSUB, are errors. A RETURN without GOSUB is generally caused by crashing through because the END statement has been omitted.

Example:

```
FOR X% = 1 TO 5
   GOSUB printit              'call to subroutine
NEXT
END
printit:                      'line name
   PRINT "Call number "; X%   'subroutine action
RETURN                        'back to caller
```

Associated with: CALL, ON...GOSUB, ON Keyword, RETURN, SUB

Points to note:

GOSUB and RETURN are provided for compatibility with older programs only. Use CALL and SUB for new programs. The SUB procedure allows for local variables and a much better isolation of the procedure from the calling program, allowing routines to be used in more than one program without alteration.

GOTO

Type:	Statement
Typical syntax:	GOTO line reference
Action:	Transfer execution of a program to another line.
Options:	None.
Argument(s):	A line number or line label name.
Restrictions:	None.

Example:

```
IF Nomen$ <> "" GOTO carryon   'test and GOTO
Nomen$ = "Default name"        'if test fails, default
carryon:                       'skip to here
Print "Name is "; Nomen$       'use name
END
```

Associated with: DEF FN, EXIT, FUNCTION, GOSUB, ON ERROR, SUB

Points to note:

GOTO should be used only as part of the ON ERROR GOTO type of event handling. It can, in a few circumstances, be used to force program execution to skip forward over several lines.

All programming languages contain some form of GOTO statement, but usually only as a last resort when there is no other way of making the execution of a program move to another position. Early versions of BASIC had very few loop forming statements, often only FOR...NEXT, so that GOTO was needed in order to create loops.

The use of GOTO along with numbered lines allowed programmers to jump to any part of a program much as the jump type of command does in assembly languages, and because many programmers who used BASIC at that time had previously used assembly language, this use of GOTO became associated with BASIC.

This led to programs which were exceedingly difficult to follow because of the jumps in position, and BASIC was condemned by academics (most of whom had never programmed in assembly language) as a language not to be taken seriously. BASIC became the most widely understood and widely used programming language for micro computers, and modern versions such as QBASIC are almost unrecognisable in comparison to the original types (some of which required only 4K for their interpreter).

Using GOTO can result in unplanned, unfathomable and unworkable programs, particularly true when GOTO is used to form loops. QBASIC is provided with a wealth of loop structures that should make the use of GOTO unnecessary for forming loops. Use EXIT to leave loops prematurely rather than a GOTO.

HEX$

Type:	Function returning string
Typical syntax:	string = HEX$(number)
Action:	Converts a number into hexadecimal form as a string.
Options:	None.
Argument(s):	The number argument, held within brackets, is an integer or long integer.
Restrictions:	Not applicable to floating-point numbers these will be rounded if used.
Example:	

```
PRINT "Address in Hex is "; HEX$(A&)
```

Associated with: OCT$, VARPTR, VARPTR$

Points to note:

To convert a hex string to denary, use VAL on a hex string that starts with the characters &H, as, for Example:

```
HX$ = "OF2C"
PRINT VAL("&H" + HX$)
```

IF

Type:	Statement
Typical syntax:	IF condition THEN statement

IF condition THEN
Statement
Statement
END IF

IF condition THEN
Statement
ELSE statement
END IF

Action: Tests for conditions being satisfied and uses THEN to indicate action.

Options: ELSE offers an alternative if the main condition fails, and the ELSE can be followed by another IF. The END IF marks the end of a block of statements started by the first IF...THEN.

Argument(s): The condition can be any test of equality or inequality.

Restrictions: IF and THEN must be on the same line. The END IF statement is used when the statement uses more than one line.

Examples:

(a) `IF A% = "XXX" THEN EXIT DO`

(b) `IF Nomen$ = END THEN`
  `    PRINT "End of List"`
  `    GOSUB sort`
  `    GOSUB print`
  `END IF`

Associated with: ELSE, END IF, THEN

Points to note:

Though very complicated IF...THEN....ELSE blocks can be constructed in QBASIC, it is usually simpler to use SELECT CASE for such actions, leaving IF...THEN for simpler tests.

As the first example shows, an IF test can be used with EXIT to form a condition for leaving a loop prematurely (that is, not at the start or at the end of the loop).

IMP

Type: Operator returning Boolean TRUE or FALSE

Typical syntax: Condition1 IMP Condition2

Action: The truth table for IMP is:

Condition1	Condition2	IMP result
FALSE	FALSE	TRUE
FALSE	TRUE	TRUE
TRUE	FALSE	FALSE
TRUE	TRUE	TRUE

Options: None.

Argument(s): Two conditions being compared.

Restrictions: Each condition must have a Boolean (TRUE/FALSE) result, and the IMP operator will produce a Boolean FALSE result only if the first condition is TRUE and the second is FALSE.

Example:

```
IF (Name$ = "") IMP (Worknr = 0) THEN GOSUB Carryon
REM False if name is blank but a number assigned
```

Associated with: AND, EQV, NOT, OR, XOR

Points to note:

It is very unusual to find this used in a program. This, like other Boolean operators, is of very low precedence. Use with numbers can produce unexpected results, see AND.

INKEY$

Type:	Function returning string
Typical syntax:	stringvariable = INKEY$
Action:	Reads the keyboard and returns a character corresponding to a pressed key. Extended keys produce two bytes, ASCII 0 and a key code number (so that INKEY$ reads two characters). If no key is pressed at the (very brief) instant when the keyboard is read, a null-string is returned.
Options:	None.
Argument(s):	None
Restrictions:	Must be used in a loop in order to detect when a key is pressed.

Examples:

(a)
```
DO K$ = INKEY$
WHILE K$ = " "
PRINT "Character is "; K$
```

(b)
```
CLS
PRINT "Press any key "
GOSUB flash
PRINT "You pressed "; K$
END
REM Uses flashing asterisk to mark position
flash:
K$ = " "                        'clear variable
DO WHILE K$ = " "               'loop condition, test K$
  K$ = INKEY$                   'look for key, store as K$
  PRINT "*";                    'asterisk on screen
  GOSUB pause                   ,wait
  PRINT CHR$(29); CHR$(32); CHR$(29); ' delete it
  GOSUB pause                   'wait
LOOP                            'back to start
RETURN
pause:
```

```
FOR N = 1 TO 500
NEXT
RETURN
```

Associated with: INPUT$, INPUT

Points to note:

The key character is not echoed on the screen. For more than one character input, INPUT$ is much more suitable and for most purposes INPUT$ would be used even for single-character responses.

INKEY$ is better suited to use in larger loops, as the second example shows. In this example, the variable K$ is assigned a null value before the loop starts, so that the loop must run at least once. The next step in the loop is to check for a key to assign to K$, and then to print an asterisk, pause, delete and pause again. This set of steps is repeated until K$ is assigned by pressing a key. The response is slow because two pause intervals must elapse between pressing a key and ending the loop, so that the routine can be improved by using an EXIT DO step when A$ is assigned by pressing a key.

If you want INKEY$ to test for extended character codes, use code such as:

```
R$ = INKEY$
IF LEN(R$) = 2 THEN…
```

to detect two-character codes.

INP

Type:	Function returning integer
Typical syntax:	variable = INP (portnumber)
Action:	Reads a byte at the specified port.
Options:	None.
Argument(s):	The number (usually in hexadecimal) of required input port, enclosed in brackets.
Restrictions:	None – it is up to the user to ensure that the argument is of a valid port.

Example:

```
LS% = INP(&H61)          'read status register
LS% = LS% AND &H00FC     'use 0000000011111100 for mask
FOR j% = 1 TO 800        'loop for loudspeaker note
LS% = LS% XOR 2          'reverse bit 1
OUT &H61, LS%            'put out
FOR N% = 1 TO 5: NEXT    'brief wait
NEXT                     'then again
END
REM causes sound by switching the loudspeaker on
REM and off rapidly in a loop
```

Associated with: AND, OUT, XOR

Points to note:

This function should be used only by programmers with a knowledge of machine code and PC design. The most common use is to read a port value and XOR the result with a number so as to toggle the value of a bit. OUT is then used to return the new value, as indicated in the example. This can be used, for example, to alter the setting of the Num Lock, Caps Shift or other keys by using the keyboard port number and the appropriate bit.

See the appropriate technical manual for your computer for details of port addresses and their uses.

INPUT

Type:	Statement
Typical syntax:	OPEN filename FOR INPUT AS number
Options:	None.
Argument(s):	None.
Restrictions:	Used only along with OPEN statement.
Action:	Opens a sequential file for input, allowing the use of the INPUT #1 type of statement.

Example:

```
OPEN "Myfile.SER" FOR INPUT AS #2
REM Opens existing file
INPUT #2, ser$            'read data string
```

Associated with: APPEND, BINARY, INPUT, OPEN, OUTPUT, RANDOM

Points to note:

Use APPEND to add data to a sequential file. APPEND will also create and open a new file if no file of the specified name exists.

INPUT

Type:	Statement
Typical syntax:	INPUT variablename, variablename, …
	INPUT prompt$; variablename, variablename,…
	INPUT; prompt$, variablename, variablename,…
	INPUT #number, data
Action:	Reads a specified type of input (number or string) from the keyboard, pausing until the ENTER key is pressed. The input is assigned to a variable. INPUT can also be used to read a file, making use of a file channel number.
Options:	Using a semi-colon immediately following INPUT causes the entry to be on the same line. A comma or a semicolon can be used to separate the prompt from the variable name.
Argument(s):	The variable to be assigned and, optionally, a string that can be used as a prompt. The file reading version requires the file channel number.
Restrictions:	The variable that is used with INPUT must be of the correct type for the data being requested. Any type of data can be assigned to a string variable, but only a number of the correct type can be assigned to a number variable. Using an incorrect response will result in the message:

Redo from start

which, despite what it says, does not mean that the program has to be restarted, only that another input, of the correct type, is required.

An input string must not contain commas unless these are used to separate several inputs on the same line. For example, INPUT A%,B% could be answered with 5,6. A string containing a comma will be regarded as two strings. Use LINE INPUT if a reply string is likely to contain a comma.

Examples:

(a) `PRINT "Type two numbers, then ENTER key"`
     `INPUT A%, B%         ' type number, comma, number, ENTER`
     `PRINT A%, B%         ' see what has been typed`

(b) `INPUT "Name?"; N$      'message and input in one line`
     `PRINT "Name is ";N$    'print input to check`

(c) `OPEN "Myfile" FOR INPUT AS #2    'open file`
     `INPUT #2, A$, B%, C#             'read items`
     `PRINT A4, B%, C#                 'print them`

(d) `INPUT; "Name is - "; N$   'keeps answer on same line`

Associated with: INKEY$, INPUT$, LINE INPUT

Points to note:

Because the Redo from Start message is so often mis-interpreted by users, it is better always to assign to a string variable and then use VAL if a number was to be input. You can then use tests of your own, placing the INPUT in a loop that will be repeated, with appropriate error messages, if the wrong kind of data is provided.

INPUT$

Type: Function

Typical syntax : variable$ = INPUT$(number)

variable$ = INPUT$(number, filehandle)

Action: Reads a specified number of string characters from the keyboard or from a file. The input characters are not echoed on the screen.

Options: A file handle number, as allocated by an OPEN statement, can be added as an argument if a file is to be read.

Argument(s): The number of characters to be supplied. If a file is to be read, the file channel number must follow the number of characters. The arguments must be enclosed in brackets and if two arguments are used they must be separated by a comma.

Restrictions: If a file read is to be performed, the file must already be open.

Example:

```
Pass$ = INPUT$(6)              'ask for password
IF Pass$ = "05qpz4"           'test it
   PRINT "Password accepted"  'accept
   GOSUB Access               'access to program
END IF
END                          'out if not correct
```

Associated with: INKEY$, INPUT, LINE INPUT

Points to note:

INPUT$(1) can be used to replace lines such as:

```
DO WHILE INKEY$ = ""
LOOP
```

which are used to wait for a key to be pressed. It can also replace the loops that assign a variable using INKEY$, such as:

```
DO
K$ = INKEY$
LOOP WHILE K$ = ""
```

in which the value of K$ will be used in a menu choice or similar action.

INSTR

Type:	Function returning integer number
Typical syntax:	INSTR (string1$, string2$)
	INSTR (number, string1$, string2$)
Action:	Returns an integer position number to show the starting position of one string inside another. The number is zero if the larger string does not contain the smaller string.
Options:	An integer start position number between INSTR and the first string can specify the starting position for searching.
Argument(s):	String1$ is the longer string which is to be searched, string2$ is the smaller string which is to be found within string1$. These arguments are not placed in brackets. If a starting position is not used, searching will start at the first character. The arguments must be enclosed in brackets and separated by a comma.
Restrictions:	The string that is being searched for must not be larger than the string that is being searched.

Example:

```
PRINT "Your answer, please (Y or N)"
DO                                 'start loop
  A$ = INPUT$(1)                   'get single letter
LOOP WHILE INSTR("YyNn", A$) = 0   'test for Y,y,N or n
PRINT "Answer is "; A$             'confirm
REM Loop continues until answer is acceptable
```

Associated with: LEFT$, MID$, RIGHT$

Points to note:
The function will return a zero if the string being searched for is longer than the string being searched.
The search is case sensitive, so that searching for NO in ignoble will not return a position.

INT

Type:	Function returning integer or long integer
Typical syntax:	J% = INT (reply#)
Action:	Returns the nearest integer or long integer value *less* than the argument.
Options:	None.
Argument(s):	Any floating-point number, variable or expression enclosed in brackets.
Restrictions:	The value of the argument must be within integer or long-integer range.

Example:

```
PRINT INT(5.66)      gives 5
PRINT INT(-73.1)     gives -74
```

Associated with: CINT, CLNG, FIX

Points to note:

Assignment of a number to an integer variable carries out this type of action. If you are assigning to an integer variable you need to be sure that the range of the number will not fall outside the permitted integer range.

IOCTL

Type:	Function
Typical syntax:	IOCTL filenumber, control$
Action:	Sends a string representing a control command to a device driver.
Options:	None.
Argument(s):	Number of open file, string of control characters.
Restrictions:	The string must be a valid command for the device.
Example:	No suitable example can be devised – only a few users will have a device (such as a modem) connected that requires such commands and which will be controlled from BASIC.

Associated with: IOCTL$

Points to note:

To be used only by machine-code programmers who are aware of the variety of control commands that can be used.

IOCTL$

Type:	(Function, Statement, Operator)
Typical syntax:	var$ = IOCTLS (filenumber)
Action:	Returns value of string returned from a device driver.
Options:	None.
Argument(s):	File channel number.
Restrictions:	None.
Example:	No suitable examples available.

Associated with: IOCTL

Points to note:

Used only where a device such as a modem can be interrogated and returns a string indicating its status.

KEY

Type:	Statement
Typical syntax:	KEY number, string
	KEY LIST
	KEY ON
	KEY OFF
Action:	Assigns strings to function keys or displays function key assignments.
Options:	In the form KEY without arguments, LIST displays key assignments. ON turns on a menu-bar of key assignments at the foot of the screen. OFF removes the menu-bar list.
Argument(s):	Key number in the range 1 to 10. String is the set of characters to be assigned to a key.
Restrictions:	When the function key list is on, the 25th line of the screen is used. This line will not scroll, and an error message will appear if you try to use LOCATE on this line. Only the first six characters of a string will appear on the menu list.

Example:

```
KEY 5, "Save file"     'message for this key
KEY ON                 'display in list
```

Associated with: KEY(number), ON KEY

Points to note:

Numbers 30 and 31 can be used for function keys F11 and F12.

For user-defined key sequences, see the other form of KEY statement following

KEY statement

Type: Statement

Typical syntax:
KEY number ON
KEY number OFF
KEY number STOP
ON KEY number GOSUB line

Action: Used to enable, disable or suspend trapping of the key-press event. When trapping is enabled, the ON KEY statement will cause a routine to be run when a nominated key is pressed.

Options: ON enables key trapping, OFF disables trapping. Using STOP will disable trapping but when trapping is enabled subsequently, and use of the trapped key in the interval will cause the GOSUB to be run.

Argument(s): Code for key, using the set:

0	All keys listed below (not used with ON KEY GOSUB).
1-10	Function keys F1-F10.
11	Up cursor key.
12	Left cursor key.
13	Right cursor key.
14	Down cursor key.
15-25	User-defined keys.
30	F11 key.
31	F12 key.

Restrictions: The code numbers shown are applicable to the old-style keyboard – see under for use with modern 101/102 key keyboards. Some key codes require Num Lock to be off.

Example:

```
ON KEY(1) GOSUB helpit
PRINT "Press F2 for Help"
KEY(1) ON
Statements
END
helpit:
PRINT " This is F1 action"
```

```
SLEEP 5
RETURN
```

Associated with: KEY statement

Points to note:

Some keys on the 101/102 type of keyboard require special treatment. The important point to remember is that the cursor key codes refer to the cursor keys on the *numeric keypad only*, not the usual set of cursor keys that lie between the main key set and the numeric keypad on a standard 101/102 key keyboard.

The numbers 15 to 25 are reserved for user-defined keys, meaning that any key or key combination can be defined as having one of these numbers. This action allows you to use any key on the keyboard, including the separate set of cursor keys, providing you know how to assign a user-defined number to these keys. Such an assignment is made by using the KEY command followed by a list of characters that carry key codes, and for this you need a list of keycodes. These are not the same as the ASCII codes that the keys normally provide. These codes are shown if Figure KEY #1.

If, for example, you need to make the code for user-defined key 15 respond to the spacebar, you would program this as:

```
KEY (15), CHR$(0) + CHR$(57)
ON KEY(15) GOSUB routine
```

since the spacebar uses code 57 in the list above. This allows you to interrupt your program by pressing the spacebar.

The first CHR$ setting of the two illustrated above is for the keyboard state. A key can be struck by itself or along with either SHIFT key, the Ctrl key, Alt, Numlock, or Caps Lock. In addition, the 101/102 key type of keyboards on modern machines contain keys that do not exist on the older types. A set of codes is therefore used for keyboard state as follows:

Value	Key state
0	No special keys
1 to 3	Either Shift key
4	Ctrl key
8	Alt key
32	NumLock key
64	Caps Lock key
128	Extended keys on a 101/102-key keyboard

You can specify more than one state by adding numbers. For example, since most PC/AT keyboards by default start up with the NumLock key on, the NumLock code of 32 can be added to any other key you want to use.

This also allows the four cursor keys on the 101/102 key set to be used, because these need the extended keyboard code of 128. If the Num Lock is set as a default, we need to add 32, so that for the up-cursor key (code 72 for the one on the number keypad) we would use:

KEY (15), CHR$(128+32) + CHR$(72)

Remember that the first CHR$ number is for the state of the keyboard and the second is for the key scan code.

Key	Code	Key	Code	Key	Code
Esc	1	A	30	Caps Lock	58
! or 1	2	S	31	F1	59
@ or 2	3	D	32	F2	60
# or 3	4	F	33	F3	61
$ or 4	5	G	34	F4	62
% or 5	6	H	35	F5	63
^ or 6	7	J	36	F6	64
& or 7	8	K	37	F7	65
* or 8	9	L	38	F8	66
(or 9	10	: or ;	39	F9	67
) or 0	11	" or '	40	F10	68
_ or -	12	~ or `	41	F11	133
+ or =	13	Left Shift	42	F12	134
Bksp	14	| or \	43	NumLock	69
Tab	15	Z	44	Scroll Lock	70
Q	16	X	45	Home or 7	71
W	17	C	46	Up or 8	72
E	18	V	47	PgUp or 9	73
R	19	B	48	Gray -	74
T	20	N	49	Left or 4	75
Y	21	M	50	Centre or 5	76
U	22	< or ,	51	Right or 6	77
I	23	> or .	52	Gray +	78
O	24	? or /	53	End or 1	79
P	25	Right Shift	54	Down or 2	80
{ or [	26	Prt Sc or *	55	PgDn or 3	81
} or]	27	Alt	56	Ins or 0	82
Enter	28	Spacebar	57	Del or .	83
Ctrl	29				

Figure KEY #1

KILL

Type:	Statement
Typical syntax:	KILL filename$
Action:	Deletes a selected file – comparable to the MS-DOS DEL command.
Options:	None.
Argument(s):	The name of the file as a string, no brackets required.
Restrictions:	An error will occur if the file does not exist.

Example:

```
KILL "C:\QBASIC\BASFILE\MYFILE.BAS"  'delete this file
KILL "C:\QBASIC\*.BAS"               'delete all BAS files
KILL "A:\*.*"                        'delete all files
```

Associated with: CHDIR, FILES, MKDIR, RMDIR

Points to note:

The wildcard characters ? and * can be used, as illustrated above.

LBOUND

Type:	Function returning integer number
Typical syntax:	LBOUND (array)
	LBOUND (array, dimension)
Action:	Returns the lowest useable subscript of a specified array.
Options:	The dimension figure is used to specify which dimension of a multi-dimensional array is to be checked. The default is 1.
Argument(s):	Array name, optionally dimension figure (usually 2 or 3, default 1). Arguments must be placed between brackets.
Restrictions:	None.

Example:

```
DIM numarr%(2 TO 20)
PRINT LBOUND (numarr%)          'gives 2
```

Associated with: DIM, REDIM, UBOUND

Points to note:

Normally, an array is declared in a program and its lower boundary is known, so that LBOUND is not a function that is much used.

LCASE$

Type: Function returning string

Typical syntax: LCASE$(string)

Action: Converts a selected string entirely to lower-case
                      letters.

Options: None.

Argument(s):   The name of the string to be converted, within
                      brackets.

Restrictions: None.

Example:

```
A$ = "ThE EnD"
PRINT LCASE$(A$)            'gives the end
```

Associated with: UCASE$

Points to note:

The main use of LCASE$ is in sorting routines in which comparisons should be made between letters of the same case, to avoid the problems of ASCII sort orders. For example the ASCII letter Z is code 90 and the letter a is code 97, so that sorting in strict ASCII order places all uppercase letters before any lowercase letter. This is avoided by using a comparison of the type:

```
IF LCASE$(A$(j%)) <= LCASE$(A$(j%+1)) THEN
   SWAP A$(j%), A$(j%+1)
END IF
```

in which the lowercase versions are compared. The strings themselves are still in lower or mixed case, only the comparison uses lower-case. It is more usual, however, to use UCASE$ for comparisons.

LEFT$

Type:	Function returning string
Typical syntax:	variable1$ = LEFT$(variable2$, number)
Action:	Copies characters from the left side of a string into another string, or to the screen or printer.
Options:	None.
Argument(s):	String from which characters are extracted, number of characters starting at lefthand side of string. Arguments are enclosed in brackets.
Restrictions:	None.

Examples:

```
(a)  A$ = LEFT$ ("MOTHERBOARD",4)   'gives MOTH in A$

(b)  N$ = "UPPER CASE"
     PRINT LEFT$(N$, 2)              'prints UP

(c)  name$ = JAMES Hardly-fair
     LPRINT (name$, 5)               'prints JAMES
```

Associated with: LTRIM$, MID$, RIGHT$, TRIM$

Points to note:

Use LTRIM$ to remove unwanted spaces from the lefthand side of a string before using LEFT$.

LEN

Type:	Function returning integer number
Typical syntax:	number = LEN(string)
	number = LEN (number variable)
Action:	Counts the number of characters in the specified string, including spaces, or shows the amount of storage space needed for a number variable.
Options:	None.
Argument(s):	String whose characters are to be counted, or number variable whose storage space is to be found, enclosed in brackets.
Restrictions:	Note that for older versions of BASIC, using LEN with a number variable would cause an error. LEN cannot be used with a number literal such as in LEN (325884.67).

Examples:

```
N$ = "The Prologue"
J% = LEN(N$)                    'find length
PRINT((80 - J%) / 2); N$        'print centred
A# = 312405.667
PRINT "Space needed for A# is "; LEN(A#)
REM Shows size of a double-precision number
```

Associated with: None

Points to note:

When a string has been formed from a number by using STR$(number), there is usually a leading space that will make the LEN number larger than the number of visible characters. This space can be removed by using LTRIM$.

LET

Type:	Statement
Typical syntax:	LET variable = value
Action:	Assigns value to variable.
Options:	None.
Argument(s):	Variable name to be assigned with value.
Restrictions:	None.

Example:

```
LET Name$ = "Sinclair"
```

Associated with: DIM

Points to note:

LET is included in QBASIC for compatibility only. LET is not used nor required in modern BASIC versions, and not required in any Microsoft BASIC since 1978.

LINE

Type:	Statement
Typical syntax:	LINE start – stop
	LINE start – stop, col, B
	LINE start – stop,, BF
	LINE start – stop,,,dotdash
Action:	A multi-use drawing statement for lines and boxes.
Options:	Colour number to establish line colour.
	B to cause a box to be drawn.
	BF for a filled box, using specified colour.
	Dotdash number to determine line type (dotted, dashed).
	STEP used ahead of each pair of co-ordinates to make them relative to present cursor position.
Argument(s):	Start and Stop co-ordinates, separated by commas. Each pair of co-ordinates must be enclosed in brackets.
Restrictions:	The Line-type number is best supplied in hexadecimal form. Commas must not be omitted if intermediate parameters are omitted.

Example:

```
LINE (20,50) - (90, 200)               'straight line
LINE (10,40) - (100,180),, B           'box
LINE (20,50) - (200,100), 11, BF, &H0F0F 'filled and pattern
```

Associated with: CIRCLE, SCREEN

Points to note:

Suitable dot dash numbers have to be devised using binary and hexadecimal. The simplest form to write is binary, using a 1 to mean a dot and 0 to mean a blank space. In this format, **1100** makes an elongated dot and space, and **11110000** makes a dash and space. The numbers that LINE uses for line type all consist of 16 binary bits (0 or 1). For example,

1010101010101010

will create a finely dotted line and

1111000011110000

will create a dashed line. The main problem is to convert these binary numbers into a form that you can type into a LINE statement, and using hexadecimal code is by far the easiest method.

Hexadecimal means scale of sixteen, and the reason that it is used so extensively is that it is naturally suited to representing binary bytes. Four bits, half of a byte, will represent numbers which lie in the range 0 to 15 in our ordinary number scale. This is the range of one hex digit.

Binary	Hex	Binary	Hex	Binary	Hex	Binary	Hex
0000	0	0100	4	1000	8	1100	C
0001	1	0101	5	1001	9	1101	D
0010	2	0110	6	1010	A	1110	E
0011	3	0111	7	1011	B	1111	F

Table STATEMENT #1

Since we don't have symbols for digits higher than 9, we have to use the letters A,B,C,D,E, and F to supplement the digits 0 to 9 in the hex scale. The advantage is that a byte can be represented by a two-digit number, and an integer by a four-digit number. Converting between binary and hex is much simpler than converting between binary and denary, using table STATEMENT #1, because a binary number can be split into four-digit groups (starting the righthand side) and each set of four binary digits converted to hex using table STATEMENT #1. The final hex number is written with the &H prefix if it is to be used in the QBASIC LINE statement.

Now the great value of hex code is how closely it corresponds to binary code. If you look at the hex-binary Table xx.x you can see that &H9 is 1001 in binary and &HF is 1111. The hex number &H9F is therefore just 10011111 in binary – you simply write down the binary digits that correspond to the hex digits. Taking another example, the hex byte &HB8 is 10111000, because &HB is 1011 and &H8 is 1000. The conversion in the opposite direction is just as easy – you group the binary digits in fours, starting at the least significant (righthand) side of the number, and then convert each group into its corresponding hex digit.

For example, the number for dotted lines that in binary is 1010101010101010 is grouped as 1010 1010 1010 1010 and in hex this is &HAAAA. The binary number 1111000011110000 similarly translates to &HF0F0, so that it becomes relatively painless to write down the binary pattern for a dot/dash line and convert to hex. This is considerably easier than using denary numbers, because a lot of these binary patterns correspond to negative integer values, and the conversion is nowhere near so simple as it is to hex.

LINE INPUT

Type: Statement

Typical syntax: LINE INPUT variable$

LINE INPUT prompt$; variable$

LINE INPUT; prompt$; variable$

LINE INPUT filenumber, variable$

Action: Reads a single string input that can contain commas.

Options: Makes the same uses of semicolons and prompts as the INPUT statement.

Argument(s):   A string variable to which typed input is assigned, a prompt if needed, a file handle number if the source of data is a file.

Restrictions: Up to 255 characters only can be input.

Examples:

(a)   ```
LINE INPUT; "Enter as Surname, forename"; Name$
REM This input can contain commas
```

(b)   ```
OPEN "Myfile" FOR INPUT AS #2     'open file
LINE INPUT #2, Newname$           'read contents
CLOSE                             'close file
```

Associated with: INKEY$, INPUT, INPUT$

Points to note:

A semicolon following the prompt causes a question mark to be printed on screen. A semicolon between LINE INPUT and the prompt keeps the reply in the same line.

LOC

Type:	Function returning integer
Typical syntax:	LOC filenumber
Action:	If the file is binary, LOC returns the position of the last byte read or written. If the file is random-access, LOC returns the number of the last record read from or written to the file. If the file is sequential LOC returns the current byte position in the file, divided by 128 (making the assumption that the file is used in 128-character blocks). For a communications file, LOC will give the number of characters in the buffer.
Options:	None
Argument(s):	The number of an open file or device, *without* the hash sign, enclosed in brackets.
Restrictions:	The editor will intercept any attempt to use the # symbol with the number that is used as the argument for LOC.

Example:

```
OPEN "Demo" FOR BINARY AS #1    'open file
A$ = "LOC Demo"                 'assign string
PUT #1, , A$                    'put in file
PRINT LOC(1)                    'print position, which is 8
CLOSE                           'close
END
```

Associated with: CLOSE, GET, OPEN, PUT

Points to note:

For a random-access file, using a record number in the PUT or GET statement allows the position in the file to be selected without the additional step of using LOC.

LOCATE

Type:	Statement
Typical syntax:	LOCATE row, column
	LOCATE row, column, visible
	LOCATE row, cursor, visible, start, stop
Action:	Moves the screen cursor to the specified position.
Options:	A cursor number can be used with the numbers
	0 = invisible *and*
	1 = visible.
	The cursor size can be altered by using a start and a stop number, both in the range 0 to 31. These numbers refer to the screen lines used for the cursor, and for a full-size cursor a range of 0 to 7 is suitable for low-resolution screens, 0 to 13 for higher resolution.
Argument(s):	Row and column position numbers; other options for making cursor visible or invisible and cursor size.
Restrictions:	Row and column numbers must be in the correct range. Note that row 25 is not available when a KEY ON menu display is being used. The range of useful numbers for start and stop depends on the screen type. If an argument is omitted between others, its comma must be inserted.

Examples:

(a)
```
LOCATE 5,50
PRINT "Here"
```

(b)
```
SCREEN 0            'text screen only
LOCATE 5,50,,0,10   'big cursor
PRINT "There"       'located
INPUT A$            'look at cursor!
```

Associated with: CSRLIN, POS

Points to note:

CSRLIN and POS can be used to find current cursor positionand store the co-ordinates as variables. These can subsequently be used in LOCATE to replace the cursor in its former position. The cursor size option applies only to the text screen and has no effect on SCREEN 12, for example.

LOCK

Type: Statement

Typical syntax: LOCK filenumber

LOCK filenumber, record

LOCK filenumber, start TO end

Action: Prevents a file from being accessed over a network.

Options: A complete file, a single record, or a range of records can be locked.

Argument (s): The Filenumber is for an open file. For a random-access file, a record number can be used to specify locking that number. Alternatively, the numbers of the first and last records of a range can be used. For a binary file either a specified numbered byte or a range of bytes can be locked.

Restrictions: Applies only to a networked machine.

Examples:

(a)   `LOCK #1,5`   `'lock Record number 5`

(b)   `LOCK #2, 2 TO 100`   `'lock these records`

(c)   `LOCK #3`   `'lock complete file`

Associated with: OPEN, UNLOCK

Points to note:
When LOCK is used on a sequential file, all records are locked.

LOF

Type:	Function returning integer or long integer
Typical syntax:	LOF(filenumber)
Action:	Returns the length of an open file as a number of bytes.
Options:	None.
Argument(s):	The file handle number for an open file, enclosed in brackets.
Restrictions:	None, any type of file can be used.

Example:

```
OPEN "Myfile" FOR BINARY AS #2
PRINT LOF(2)
CLOSE
```

Associated with: OPEN

Points to note:

Some older BASIC varieties could use LOF on a serial file but the returned number was of little use.

LOG

Type:	Function returning double-precision number
Typical syntax:	LOG (numbervariable)
Action:	Finds natural (Naperian) logarithm of a number.
Options:	None.
Argument(s):	The number, variable or expression whose natural logarithm is to be found, enclosed in brackets.
Restrictions:	The argument must not be zero or negative – this gives an *Illegal Function Call*, Error 5.

Examples:

(a)
```
PRINT "Power of 2 to find (up to 16)"
INPUT A%
PRINT "2 ^ ";A%; " is "; EXP (LOG(2) * A%)
```

(b)
```
PRINT "Input the ratio of voltages"
INPUT x
PRINT "Db ratio is "; (LOG(X) / 2.3026) * 20
```

Associated with: ATAN, COS, EXP, SIN, TAN

Points to note:

The Naperian logarithm uses base e (EXP) rather than the base 10 for ordinary logarithms; it was the first form of logarithm to be discovered (by Napier in 1614), and the principles were used to make rods which were used (like a slide-rule) for multiplications. To find the anti-logarithm, use EXP. The relationship is:

```
K = LOG (A)
A = EXP (K)
```

The relationship between the Naperian logarithm and the common (base 10) logarithm is:

```
Common LOG = Naperian log / Naperian LOG(10)
```

– the value of Naperian LOG(10) is approximately 2.3026, as used in the second example above.

If base 10 logarithms are to be used extensively, as they are in several calculations in science and engineering, a defined function can be used to carry out the conversion.

LOOP

Type: Statement

Typical syntax: LOOP

LOOP UNTIL condition

LOOP WHILE condition

Action: Repeats a set of statements headed by the DO statement.

Options: LOOP used with UNTIL will loop until the condition is true (while the condition is false). LOOP used with WHILE will loop while the condition is true (until the condition is false).

Argument(s): None

Restrictions: Used only with DO to mark the start of the loop. If neither DO nor LOOP lines contain any conditions the loop will be infinite unless it contains an EXIT DO clause.

Examples:

(a)
```
DO                              'start loop
N% = N% + 1                     'counter
INPUT Name$(N%)                 'data input
LOOP UNTIL N% = 100 OR UCASE$(Name$(N%)) = "END"
REM Two possible loop ending clauses using UNTIL
```

(b)
```
DO                              'start loop
N% = N% + 1                     'counter
INPUT Name$(N%)                 'data input
LOOP WHILE N% < 100 OR UCASE$(Name$(N%)) <> "END"
REM Two possible loop ending clauses using WHILE
```

Associated with: DO, EXIT DO

Points to note:

Using UNTIL or WHILE along with LOOP tests the condition(s) at the end of the loop, so that the loop will run at least once even if the condition for ending it is true. See DO for testing at the start of the loop.

The choice of WHILE or UNTIL allows conditions to be formulated so as to avoid awkward negatives, because WHILE TRUE is equivalent to UNTIL FALSE and WHILE FALSE is equivalent to UNTIL TRUE. Compare the ending conditions in the example to see how this can make one form preferable to the other.

LPOS

Type:	Function returning integer number
Typical syntax:	LPOS (Portnumber)
Action:	Returns the number of characters sent to the printer since the last carriage return. It can therefore be used to determine when a cariage return is sent.
Options:	None.
Argument (s):	The port number is 0 for LPT1, 1 for LPT2, 2 for LPT3 and 3 for LPT4. The argument must be enclosed in brackets.
Restrictions:	Should be used only on text that has been formatted for sending to a printer.

Example:

```
PRINT "Please switch printer on line"
PRINT "Press any key when ready"
K$ = INPUT$(1)
pwid% = 80                  'characters per line
FOR j% = 32 TO 255          'ASCII range
PRINT CHR$(j%)              'on screen
LPRINT CHR$(j%)            'to printer
IF LPOS(1) >= pwid% THEN    'paper RHS reached
  LPRINT CHR$(13) + CHR$(10) 'carriage return and line feed
END IF
NEXT
END
```

Associated with: LPRINT

Points to note:

You must be sure that your printer is set so that the width number used in the test (see example) is suitable. For example, if you use the routine to send a carriage return and line feed after 132 characters you will have to make certain that the printer has been set to its condensed print mode by using a line such as:

LPRINT CHR$ (15)

which will set any Epson-compatible printer into condensed print mode. This is cancelled by using LPRINT CHR$(18).

LPRINT

Type: Statement

Typical syntax:
LPRINT item
LPRINT item;
LPRINT item, item …
LPRINT item ; item …

Action: Prints numbers or strings to the printer connected to LPT1.

Options: The use of commas to print in 14-character zones, and the semicolon to avoid taking a new line for each LPRINT, are identical to their use in PRINT statements. LPRINT can be used to print variables, literals (such as "STRING" ,22, 56,778), or the results of expressions.

Argument(s): The variables, number or string, or literals to be printed. No brackets are required.

Restrictions: A printer must be connected, switched on and put on line. If no line-feed/carriage return characters are put into long text, the printer will carry out this action at its default setting (usually 80 characters width). There is no LPRINT #2 type of statement.

Examples:

(a)
```
LPRINT A$;
LPRINT B$          'B$ is printed on same line as A$
```

(b)
```
A# = 213.7782
c% = 4
d = 27.5
LPRINT (A# * c% + d)    'prints result
```

(c)
```
C$ = "Name"
LPRINT C$ + " of item." 'prints whole phrase
```

Associated with: PRINT, LPRINT USING

Points to note:
Following a printed item with a semicolon keeps printing in the same line when a new LPRINT statement is used. Following a printed item with a comma will move the printer head to the next zone, using 14-character print zones. There is no option to alter zone widths.

LPRINT USING

Type:	Statement
Typical syntax:	LPRINT USING format$, datalist
Action:	Prints hard copy with numbers or text formatted by the format string.
Options:	Items on the data list can be separated by semicolons or commas. Using a semicolon keeps printing in the same line when a new LPRINT line is used, using a commas moves printing to the next 14-character zone.

The characters that can be used in formatting strings are divided into string field characters and number field characters.

String fields: Backslash characters are used as markers to define the size of a field to contain a string – the size of the field is the size of the space defined by the backslashes and the spaces between them. For Example:

```
"\      \"
```

contains six spaces, making a total field width of eight characters. A string defined as

```
"\\"
```

will allow the first two characters of a string to be printed in a field, and using

```
"!"
```

allows only one character, the first. Conversely, using

```
"&"
```

allows all of the characters of a string to be printed.

Number fields: Each digit of a number can be represented by a hash sign, #. Characters such as commas, decimal point and currency symbols can be placed in their correct position in relation to the digits, for example:

```
"+###.##"
```

defines a + sign, three digits ahead of the decimal point and two digits following the decimal point. A sign (+ or -) can be positioned before or following a number by placing the sign ahead or following the hash marks.

The currency sign can be placed ahead of the hashmarks, but only the dollar sign can be *floated* meaning that it will be placesd just ahead of a number of any size. For example:

LPRINT USING "$###,###.##"; 12.66

will produce:

$ 12.66

but when a double-dollar sign is used, one dollar sign will appear closed up against the first figure, so that:

LPRINT USING "$$###,###.##"; 12.66

will produce:

$12.66

– but this facility is not available for any other currency sign.

Asterisk signs are used to replace leading spaces in a number, a device often used in cheque printing to avoid forgery. For Example:

LPRINT USING "##.##";6.772**

will produce:

***6.77

– note that only two decimal places are used because of the formatting string.

The currency sign and asterisk can be combined, so that:

LPRINT USING "£###.##"; 5.32**

will produce:

£****5.32

A comma can be placed ahead of a decimal point in a formatting string to indicate that digits should be grouped in threes, so that:

LPRINT USING "######'.##"; 12176.55

will give:

12,176.55

Another special sign is the set of four carets (^^^^) which is used to indicate that a number should be formatted in scientific notation. For example:

```
LPRINT USING "#.###^^^^" 1268
```

will produce:

1.268E3

Finally, using an underscore character ahead of any formatting character will cause that character to be printed as such, not causing a formatting effect.

```
LPRINT USING _###.##"; 12.66
```

gives:

#12.66

Argument(s): The formatting string and the item list for printing.

Restrictions: The floating dollar formatting string cannot easily be adapted to use any other currency symbol. If a number value is too large to fit into its specified field, a % sign will be printed ahead of the output to draw attention to the problem. There is no LPRINT USING string #2 type of file statement.

Examples:

(a) string fields

```
CLS
name$ = "Fielding, Henry"        'string to print
LPRINT USING "\   \"; name$      'selects 5 characters
f$ = "\        \"                'longer field
LPRINT USING f$; name$           'used here
LPRINT USING "!"; name$          'single character
LPRINT USING "&"; name$          'whole string
END
```

(b) number fields

```
CLS
FOR n% = 1 TO 5              'five different formats
   RESTORE forms            'get start of formats
   FOR x% = 1 TO n%         'read the
      READ f$               'format strings
```

```
   NEXT                    'for use
   RESTORE nums            'now the numbers
   FOR j% = 1 TO 5         'five of them
      READ d               'read in
      PRINT USING f$; d    'and formatted
   NEXT                    'with one format string
   SLEEP 2                 'wait
   PRINT                   'blank line
NEXT 'next format
END
forms:
DATA"##,###.##","##.#","#,###.#","#.#","#####"
nums:
DATA 1.57,11.236,10143.2,1071623,237.145
```

Associated with: PRINT, LPRINT

Points to note:

Though a floating dollar sign can be used, there is no floating pound (or any other currency) sign, making the statement rather less useful in this respect unless you have a machine-code memory-resident program that will intercept printer calls and convert a dollar sign into a pound sign.

LSET

Type: Statement

Typical syntax: LSET fieldstring = assigned string

Action: Places data to the lefthand side of a fixed-length string in a memory buffer and pads out the space with blanks. Used in filling fields for random access filing (old system).

Options: None.

Argument(s): The fieldstring is the string that was defined in a FIELD statement for holding data in a record. This is assigned with the data from another string, usually obtained by way of an INPUT statement.

Restrictions: Either LSET or RSET must be used to assign data to a random-access field in this system, no other form of assignment can be used.

Example:

```
FILE% = 1                  'file handle
LIMIT% = 100               'set limit
OPEN "integer.rnd" FOR RANDOM AS #FILE% LEN = 2
FIELD FILE%, 2 AS A$       'two-byte string records
FOR N% = 1 TO LIMIT%       'string filling
INPUT "Integer, please"; A%    'get number
LSET A$ = MKI$(A%)         'put into buffer
PUT FILE%                  'and save
NEXT
CLOSE
REM  The PUT actions places data in the buffer, but
REM it is not saved to the disk until either the
REM buffer is full or the CLOSE statement is used.
```

Associated with: CVD, CVI, CVL, CVS, FIELD, MKD$, MKI$, MKL$, MKS$, RSET

Points to note:

This is an obsolete statement retained for the sake of compatibility. New programs should use a defined type in place of FIELD, LSET and RESET statements, avoiding the conversion functions also. A conversion program can be written to read items using the old statement and write a new file using the modern equivalents.

LTRIM$

Type:	Function returning string
Typical syntax:	variablestring = LTRIM$(string)
Action:	Removes spaces at the start of a string (leading spaces).
Options:	None.
Argument(s):	The argument can be a string or string expression contained within brackets.
Restrictions:	LTRIM$ cannot remove unwanted spaces within the string.

Example:

```
K$ = "        Ian Sinclair"     'contains spaces
PRINT K$
K$ = LTRIM$(K$)                 'removes spaces from K$
PRINT K$
```

Associated with: RTRIM$, STR$

Points to note:

LTRIM$ is particularly useful when STR$ has been used to convert a number into string form. This conversion always allows a leading space to accommodate a – (negative) sign, but if the number is not negative this space is empty and can be removed. This can be done in one operation using:

```
num$ = LTRIM$(STR$(number))
```

MID$ function

Type:	Function returning string
Typical syntax:	Stringslice = MID$(string, start, size)
Action:	Copies a portion of a string into a string variable, using a starting position counted from the start of the string, and a stated number of characters.
Options:	None.
Argument(s):	The string to be sliced, its starting position and (optionally) the number of characters, all within brackets. If the number of characters is not stated, slicing continues to the end of the string, making this equivalent to the RIGHT$ action.
Restrictions:	The start number can be in the range 1 to 32767 and the size number can be in the range 0 to 32767. If the start number is more than the string length, a null string is returned.

Example:

```
CLS
INPUT "Your name please"; nam$        'get string
L% = LEN(nam$)                        'find length
C% = L% / 2 + 1                       'get half-way
FOR N% = 1 TO C%                      'start pyramid
PRINT TAB(45 - N%); MID$(nam$, C% - N% + 1, N% * 2 - 1)
NEXT
REM Extracts letters in groups to form a letter-
REM Pyramid.
```

Associated with: LEFT$, MID$ statement, RIGHT$

Points to note:

MID$ is a more general string-slicing function that can cary out the actions of both LEFT$ and RIGHT$. It is particularly useful in statements that can employ variables for the position number and number of characters in the MID$ function.

MID$ statement

Type:	Statement
Typical syntax:	MID$(string, start, length) = newstring
Action:	Replaces a selected portion of a string with characters from another string.
Options:	None.
Argument(s):	The string variable to be altered, start position, number of changed characters, all within brackets.
Restrictions:	The string length is *never* altered by this statement. If the size number is omitted, as many characters as possible of the replacement string will be used.
	The start number can be in the range 1 to 32767, and the size number can be in the range 0 to 32767.

Example:

```
nam$ = "Service Manager is Jim   "   '6 spaces used
num$ = " Ext. 224"
PRINT nam$ + num$                    'see it
SLEEP 1                              'wait
MID$(nam$, 20) = "Neville"           'longer word
PRINT nam$ + num$                    'see it
SLEEP 1                              'wait
MID$,20) = "Leopardiusovitch"        'this is chopped
PRINT nam$ + num$                    'no extra string length
SLEEP 1
END
```

Associated with: LEFT$, MID$ function, RIGHT$

Points to note:

This action must be used carefully to avoid corrupting data. It is not used in older versions of BASIC.

MKD$

Type:	Function returning eight-character string
Typical syntax:	data$ = MKD$(number#)
Action:	Converts a double-precision number into an 8-character string for use with random-access filing using the FIELD statement.
Options:	None.
Argument(s):	A double-precision number or expression that yields a double-precision number, all within brackets.
Restrictions:	Used only with the older system of random-access filing.

Example:

```
OPEN "Randfil.RND" FOR RANDOM AS #2    'open file
A# = 213348.945                        'DP number
FIELD 8 AS data$                       'space for data
LSET(data$) = MKD$(A#)                 'convert and pack
PUT #2, data$                          'put in file
CLOSE                                  'close it
```

Associated with: CVD, CVI, CVL, CVS, FIELD, LSET, MKI$, MKL$, MKS$, RSET

Points to note:

Use for compatibility only. New programs should use a defined type (record) in place of FIELD, LSET, MKD$ and all the rest.

MKI$

Type: Function returning two-character string

Typical syntax: data$ = MKI$(number%)

Action: Converts an integer number into a two character string for random-access filing using the FIELD statement.

Options: None.

Argument(s): An integer number or expression yielding an integer, all within brackets.

Restrictions: Used only with the older system of random-access filing.

Example:

```
OPEN "Randfil.RND" FOR RANDOM AS #2    'open file
A% = 21                                'integer number
FIELD 2 AS data$                       'space for data
LSET(data$) = MKI$(A%)                 'convert and pack
PUT #2, data$                          'put in file
CLOSE                                  'close it
```

Associated with: CVD, CVI, CVL, CVS, FIELD, LSET, MKD$, MKL$, MKS$, RSET

Points to note:

Use for compatibility only. New programs should use a defined type (record) in place of FIELD, LSET, MKD$ and all the rest.

MKL$

Type:	Function returning four-character string
Typical syntax:	data$ = MKL$(number&)
Action:	Converts a long integer number into a four-character string for random-access filing using FIELD statement.
Options:	None.
Argument(s):	A long integer number or expression that yields a long integer, all within brackets.
Restrictions:	Used only with the older system of random-access filing.

Example:

```
OPEN "Randfil.RND" FOR RANDOM AS #2    'open file
A& = 2166437                           'long integer number
FIELD 4 AS data$                       'space for data
LSET(data$) = MKI$(A&)                 'convert and pack
PUT #2, data$                          'put in file
CLOSE                                  'close it
```

Associated with: CVD, CVI, CVL, CVS, FIELD, LSET, MKD$, MKI$, MKS$, RSET

Points to note:

Use for compatibility only if required. Older versions of BASIC did not usually permit the use of long integers. New programs should use a defined type (record) in place of FIELD, LSET, MKD$ and all the rest.

MKS$

Type:	Function returning four-character string
Typical syntax:	data$ = MKS$(number!)
Action:	Converts a single-precision number into a four-character string for random-access
Argument(s):	A single-precision number or expression yielding a single-precision number, all within brackets.
Restrictions:	Used only with the older system of random-access filing.

Example:

```
OPEN "Randfil.RND" FOR RANDOM AS #2   'open file
A = 21.667                            'SP number
FIELD 4 AS data$                      'space for data
LSET(data$) = MKS$(A)                 'convert and pack
PUT #2, data$                         'put in file
CLOSE                                 'close it
```

Associated with: CVD, CVI, CVL, CVS, FIELD, LSET, MKD$, MKI$, MKL$, RSET

Points to note:

Use for compatibility only. New programs should use a defined type (record) in place of FIELD, LSET, MKD$ and all the rest.

MKDIR

Type:	Statement
Typical syntax:	MKDIR name$
Action:	Creates a new directory from the current directory, or on a path stipulated in the statement.
Options:	None.
Argument(s):	Name of new directory as a string, variable or literal.
Restrictions:	If the named directory already exists, the program will stop with an Illegal Function Call, ERROR 5.

Examples:

(a) `MKDIR "NEWDIR" ' Makes NEWDIR branch from current directory`

(b) `MKDIR "C:\QBASIC\BASFILES" 'creates new directory`
`REM branching from C:\QBASIC`

(c) `MKDIR A$   'uses variable rather than literal`
`REM variable must have been assigned`

Associated with: CHDIR, FILES, KILL, RMDIR

Points to note:

If you use MKDIR in a program, set up an error handler (see ON ERROR) so that if you specify a name that already exists you will be informed and asked to try again.

MKDMBF$

Type:	Function returning eight-character string
Typical syntax:	String = MKDMBF$(number#)
Action:	Converts a number in IEEE format to the older Microsoft form of string for use with the FIELD statement.
Options:	None.
Argument(s):	A double-precision number, or an expression yielding a double-precision number, in modern IEEE format and within brackets.
Restrictions:	Use only in conjunction with random-access data files created by older versions of BASIC using Microsoft Binary Format.

Example:

```
GOSUB openoldfile          'open old random file
A# = 2133487.593           'DP number, IEEE format
LSET stor$ = MKDMBF$(a#)    'convert and pack
PUT #2, stor$              'file it
CLOSE
REM Assume that the subroutine contains the
REM FIELD statement.
```

Associated with: MKSMBF$, CVDMBF, CVSMBF

Points to note:

QBASIC uses floating point (single and double) numbers in IEEE form, and this affects the coded version produced by MKD$. Older versions of BASIC used another format, Microsoft Binary Format, and to ensure correct conversion of random-access file data from old files, the CVDMBF function should be used when reading such files with QBASIC. Similarly, in adding data to old files using a QBASIC program, the MKDMBF$ function must be used to ensure compatibility. It is preferable to use these routines only in a short program that will open the old file and also open a new file, reading from the old file using CVDMBF and CVSMBF and writing to the new one using a user-defined record type.

MKSMBF$

Type:	Function returning four-character string
Typical syntax:	String = MKSMBF$(number!)
Action:	Converts a number in modern IEEE format to Microsoft form of string for use with the FIELD statement.
Options:	None.
Argument(s):	A single-precision number, or an expression yielding a single-precision number, in modern IEEE format and enclosed in brackets.
Restrictions:	Use only in conjunction with random-access data files created by older versions of BASIC using Microsoft Binary Format.

Example:

```
GOSUB openfile              'open old random file'
A = 487.93                  'SP number, IEEE format'
L Set Stor$ = MKSMBF$ (A)   'convert and pack
PUT #2, stor$               'file it
CLOSE
REM Assume that the subroutine contains the
REM FIELD statement.
```

Associated with: MKDMBF$, CVDMBF, CVSMBF

Points to note:

QBASIC uses floating point (single and double) numbers in IEEE form, and this affects the coded version produced by MKS$. Older versions of BASIC used another format, Microsoft Binary Format, and to ensure correct conversion of random-access file data from old files, the CVSMBF function should be used when reading such files with a QBASIC program. Similarly, in adding data to old files with a QBASIC program, the MKSMBF$ function must be used to ensure compatibility. It is preferable to use these routines only in a short program that will open the old file and also open a new file, reading from the old file using CVSMBF and CVDMBF and writing to the new one using a user-defined record type.

MOD

Type:	Operator returning integer
Typical syntax:	remainder = number1 MOD number2
Action:	Returns the remainder of dividing first number by second number.
Options:	None.
Argument(s):	Two numbers, either integers or float, one on each side of the operator. The first number is divided by the second and the remainder returned.
Restrictions:	Floating point numbers will be chopped to integers.

Example:

```
S% = 26125          'time in seconds
min% = S% \ 60      'integer division
sec% = S% MOD 60    'remainder
hr% = min% \ 60     'integer division
mn% = min% MOD 60   'remainder
PRINT "Time interval is ";
PRINT hr%;":";mn%;":";sec%
```

Associated with: Integer division operator (\).

Points to note:

The use of MOD allows integer arithmetic and long-integer arithmetic to be done with prefect precision, using division that produces a quotient and a remainder rather than a floating-point number. It is particularly useful for quantities such as time which are not usually expressed using decimals. Another useful application is to arithmetic using Imperial measures.

NAME

Type:	Statement
Typical syntax:	NAME oldfile$ AS newfile$
Action:	Renames a file in any drive or directory, or copies a file to another drive or directory.
Options:	None.
Argument(s):	Valid filenames, in string form, for an existing file and its new name.
Restrictions:	A file can be renamed or it can be copied to another directory using this statement, but not both simultaneously. In other words, the actions:

```
NAME "OLDFILE.BAS" AS "NEWFILE.BAS"
NAME "C:'QBASIC'OLDFILE.BAS" AS "C:'BASFILES'OLDFILE.BAS"
```

are both valid, but

```
NAME "C:\QBASIC\OLDFILE.BAS" AS "C:\BASFILES\NEWFILE.BAS"
```

is not

Example:

```
NAME C:\QBASIC\MYFILE. BAS AS C:\QBASIC\EXAMPLE. BAS
```

Associated with: CHDIE, FILES, MKDIR, RMDIR

Points to note:

The filenames can be represented by string variables which have been assigned earlier. The filenames must obey MS-DOS rules, using up to eight characters (starting with a letter) in the main name and up to three in an optional extension.

NEXT

Type:	Statement
Typical syntax:	(a) FOR count = A TO B STEP C
	Statement
	NEXT
	(b) IF condition RESUME NEXT
Action:	(a) Terminates a FOR loop, incrementing the counter and returning to the FOR portion so that the counter value can be tested.
	(b) Terminates error trapping, causing the program to resume on the instruction following the one that caused the error.
Options:	None.
Argument(s):	In a FOR loop, the NEXT can use the variable name as an argument forming a reminder of which loop is being ended. If the name is not that used by the last-started loop, an error will result.
	The RESUME NEXT construction takes no arguments.
Restrictions:	Used only along with FOR or RESUME

Examples:

(a)
```
FOR j% = 1 TO 100 STEP 2
PRINT NAME$(j%)
NEXT
```

(b)
```
IF ERR = 42 RESUME NEXT
```

Associated with: ERL, ERR, FOR, ON ERROR

Points to note:

NEXT can be used along with a list of variables when a set of nested loops end in succession. For example, a routine which multiplies elements of a matrix can be written as:

```
matmult:
FOR h% = 1 TO n1%
  FOR j% = 1 TO n2%
    c(h%, j%) = 0
    FOR k% = 1 TO n3%
```

```
        c(h%, j%) = c(h%, j%) + a(h%, k%) * b(k%, h%)
      NEXT k%
    NEXT j%
  NEXT h%'â)p-í*í*'å
  RETURN
```

but the last four lines could be abbreviated to:

```
      NEXT k%,j%,h%
      RETURN
```

This assumes that the nesting is correct.

If the nesting is incorrect in such a set of loops, the NEXT without FOR error will be delivered and the program will stop.

NOT

Type:	Operator returning Boolean TRUE or FALSE
Typical syntax:	NOT (Boolean statement)
Action:	Provides an inverse of any expression that can be resolved to a Boolean TRUE or FALSE.
Options:	None.
Argument(s):	A Boolean expression within brackets.
Restrictions:	Should not normally be used with an argument that consists of a number alone because the NOT action is bitwise and the action can appear confusing.

Examples:

(a)
```
IF NOT (J% = 6) THEN GOSUB count
REM Test J% = 6 for TRUE or FALSE
```

(b)
```
IF NOT (Age = 27 AND Name = "Smith")
GOSUB reject
REM Makes two TRUE or FALSE tests
```

Associated with: AND, EQV, IMP, OR, XOR

Points to note:

Confusing results can be obtained when NOT is used on an expression that provides a number other than -1 or 0. This does not mean an expression such as (J% = 6), which is a true Boolean expression that must be either TRUE or FALSE, coded as -1 or 0 respectively.

The use of NOT with a pure number argument must be avoided because NOT will operate on each bit of the binary equivalent of the number. For example, NOT (8) is 7 because, in binary, 8 is 1000 and 7 is 0111 which is the number which has each bit the inverse of the corresponding bit of 1000. The same result, incidentally, will be obtained from NOT(6.6) because the operator ignores floating-point numbers and rounds down to the nearest integer.

The use of NOT can cause some problems when programs are being converted from another version of BASIC. In some versions, the argument of NOT can be any variable, so that statements such as NOT (A$) are valid, returning a 0 for a blank string A$. This type of use is undesirable, and in QBASIC any attempt to use a string variable by itself in a NOT bracket will be rejected by the Editor. You can, however, use a number variable, with the type of results discussed above, or any form of Boolean expression which can be resolved as FALSE or TRUE.

OCT$

Type:	Function returning string
Typical syntax:	string = OCT$(number)
Action:	Converts the number argument into a string that represents the octal (scale of eight) equivalent.
Options:	None.
Argument(s):	Any number, preferably an integer or long integer, within brackets. Any floating-point number within the long-integer range will be converted to an integer, short or long.
Restrictions:	There will be an error message if the number is beyond the range of a long integer.

Example:

```
PRINT OCT$ (64)     'gives 80
```

Associated with: HEX$

Points to note:

Seldom used nowadays even by programmers, and available in QBASIC more for current use. To convert from octal to denary form, use VAL on the octal string that starts with the characters &O, as, for Example:

```
OC$ = "1314"
PRINT VAL("&O" + OC$)
```

OFF

Type: Statement

Typical syntax: (a)   trap_event OFF

                     (b)   KEY OFF

Action: Disables error trapping or function key assignment displays.

Options: None.

Argument(s):   Preceded by the name of the event whose trapping is to be turned off, or by KEY when the function key display is to be turned off.

Restrictions: Used only in conjunction with KEY, COM, PEN, PLAY, STRIG and TIMER.

Examples:

(a)   `TIMER OFF`   `'turns off timer trapping`

(b)   `KEY OFF`   `'turns off key trapping`

Associated with: ON (KEY, COM, PEN, PLAY, STRIG, TIMER), STOP

Points to note:

Using OFF disables event trapping; STOP is used to suspend trapping. When an event occurs during the time when STOP is effective, the trapping will occur only when ON has been used.

ON

Type:	Statement
Typical syntax:	(a) trapevent ON
	(b) KEY ON
	(c) ON item GOTO line, line, line,...
	(d) ON item GOSUB line, line, line,...
Action:	(i) Enables error trapping or function key assignment displays.
	(ii) Selects from a list of actions when used with number argument and GOTO or GOSUB.
Options:	None.
Argument(s):	Preceded by event whose trapping is to be turned on, or by KEY when function key display is to be turned on. For menu use, an item number is used to count the list of line positions for use by GOTO or GOSUB.
Restrictions:	The trapping action is used only in conjunction with KEY, COM, PEN, PLAY, STRIG and TIMER. The menu action is used only with GOTO or GOSUB.

Examples:

(a)
```
TIMER ON              'start timer trapping
KEY ON                'display function key assignments
```

(b)
```
INPUT "Select by number, 1 to 4", N%   'get item number
ON N% GOSUB open, process, sort, leave 'use to select
REM Input 1 leads to subroutine open
REM Input 2 leads to subroutine process
REM and so on.
```

Associated with: GOTO, GOSUB, OFF (KEY, COM, PEN, PLAY, STRIG, TIMER), STOP

Points to note:

The event trapping action is also used in expressions such as ON COM, ON ERR (see later) to provide instructions for processing an event. Note the difference between the forms STRIG ON (enabling) and ON STRIG (detailing instructions). The ON GOTO and ON GOSUB form for menus are now obsolescent; use SELECT CASE for new programs.

ON COM

Type:	Statement
Typical syntax:	ON COM (number) GOSUB line
Action:	Provides a routine to use when an event is trapped at a serial port usually this provides for saving a message when an input is detected.
Options:	None.
Argument(s):	Number of Com port (1 to 4), enclosed in brackets.
Restrictions:	Trapping of the event must have been enabled by using COM ON, and the port must have been opened for use (see OPEN COM) if it is to be read or written as a file. No OPEN COM is needed to report port use only.

Examples:

(a)   Report input only

```
COM(2) ON                    'My COM1 is used by mouse
ON COM (2) GOSUB readport 'routine for COM2
PRINT "Press any key to stop"   'how to escape
DO WHILE INKEY$ = ""         'start loop
LOOP                         'until event or key pressed
COM(2) OFF                   'end trapping

readport:                    'detect
PRINT "Message received"     'character at port
RETURN                       'but do not read it
```

(b)   Prints received file

```
ON COM(2) GOSUB getinput        'use COM2
COM(2) ON                       'activate
OPEN "com2:" FOR RANDOM AS #1   'open
DO WHILE INKEY$ = ""            'infinite
PRINT combuf$                   'loop
LOOP                            'until key or message
END

getinput:                       'COM routine
INPUT #1, combuf$               'get a line
```

```
RETURN                              'that's all
REM Do not confuse #1 for handle (buffer) number
REM with the use of 2 as COM port number
```

Associated with: OPEN COM

Points to note:

The COM port must be physically present and connected to another machine either directly or by way of a modem.

ON ERROR

Type: Statement

Typical syntax: ON ERROR GOTO routine
                        ON ERROR RESUME NEXT

Action: The GOTO form branches to the line indicated by
                        label name or number when any run-time error
                        occurs. The normal error-message is suppressed.
                        When RESUME NEXT is used, the program continues
                        at the next line instead of stopping with an error
                        message or running an error routine.

Options: GOTO or RESUME, depending on whether an error-
                        routine is to be used or not.

Argument(s):   GOTO followed by routine label name, or RESUME
                        NEXT.

Restrictions: ON ERROR does not permit the use of GOSUB or
                        CALL, only GOTO or RESUME NEXT. Contrast this
                        with other ON statements which use GOSUB but not
                        GOTO.

Examples:

(a) **ON ERROR GOTO handler**   `'branches to error routine`

(b) **ON ERROR RESUME NEXT**   `'ignores line that caused error`

Associated with: ERDEV, ERDEV$, ERR, ERL, ERROR, GOTO,
                      RESUME

Points to note:

Errors such as syntax or static array dimensioning are picked up by the
editor before a program is run, only run-time errors are dealt with by ON
ERROR. More details of error handling routines can be found under the
ERR, ERROR and RESUME headings.

ON KEY

Type:	Statement
Typical syntax:	ON KEY (number) GOSUB line
Action:	Provides a routine to use when one of the trapped keys is pressed.
Options:	None.
Argument(s):	Number of KEY in range 1 to 31.

1-10	Function keys F1-10.
11	Up Cursor key.
12	Left Cursor key.
13	Right Cursor key.
14	Down Cursor key.
15-25	User-defined keys.
30, 31	Function keys F11 and F12.

Restrictions:	Trapping of the event must have been enabled by using KEY ON.

Example:

```
CLS
KEY(1) ON                 'allow trapping
ON KEY (1) GOSUB message  'routine to use
FOR n% = 1 TO 200         'loop starts
  PRINT n%
  FOR j = 1 TO 500: NEXT  'slow it down
NEXT
END
message:                  'when F1 pressed
CLS                       'this routine runs
LOCATE 5, 10              'place cursor
PRINT "Your program is still working" 'message
SLEEP 1                   'delay
CLS
RETURN                    'back
```

Associated with: KEY, ON, OFF, STOP

Points to note:

Note that this routine permits the use of GOSUB but not GOTO.

Some keys on the 101/102 type of keyboard require special treatment. The important point to remember is that the cursor key codes refer to the cursor keys on the *numeric keypad only,* not the usual set of cursor keys that lie between the main key set and the numeric keypad on a standard 101/102 key keyboard.

The numbers 15 to 25 are reserved for user-defined keys, meaning that any key or key combination can be defined as having one of these numbers. This action allows you to use any key on the keyboard, including the separate set of cursor keys, providing you know how to assign a user-defined number to these keys. Such an assignment is made by using the KEY command followed by a list of characters that carry key codes, and for this you need a list of keycodes. These are not the same as the ASCII codes that the keys normally provide. These codes are shown in Table ON KEY #1.

If, for example, you need to make the code for user-defined key 15 respond to the spacebar, you would program this as:

```
KEY (15), CHR$(0) + CHR$(57)
ON KEY(15) GOSUB routine
```

since the spacebar uses code 57 in the table overleaf. This allows you to interrupt your program by pressing the spacebar.

The first CHR$ setting of the two illustrated above is for the keyboard state. A key can be struck by itself or along with either SHIFT key, the Ctrl key, Alt, Numlock, or Caps Lock. In addition, the 101/102 key type of keyboards on modern machines contain keys that do not exist on the older types. A set of codes is therefore used for keyboard state as follows:

Value	Key state
0	No special keys.
1 to 3	Either Shift key.
4	Ctrl key.
8	Alt key.
32	NumLock key.
64	Caps Lock key.
128	Extended keys on a 101/102-key keyboard.

You can specify more than one state by adding numbers. For example, since most PC/AT keyboards by default start up with the Num Lock key on, the NumLock code of 32 can be added to any other key you want to use.

This also allows the four cursor keys on the 101/102 key set to be used, because these need the extended keyboard code of 128. If the Num Lock is set as a default, we need to add 32, so that for the up-cursor key (code 72 for the one on the number keypad) we would use:

KEY (15), CHR$(128 + 32) + CHR$(72)

Remember that the first CHR$ number is for the state of the keyboard and the second is for the key scan code.

Key	Code	Key	Code	Key	Code
Esc	1	A	30	Caps Lock	58
! or 1	2	S	31	F1	59
@ or 2	3	D	32	F2	60
# or 3	4	F	33	F3	61
$ or 4	5	G	34	F4	62
% or 5	6	H	35	F5	63
^ or 6	7	J	36	F6	64
& or 7	8	K	37	F7	65
* or 8	9	L	38	F8	66
(or 9	10	: or ;	39	F9	67
) or 0	11	" or '	40	F10	68
_ or -	12	~ or `	41	F11	133
+ or =	13	Left Shift	42	F12	134
Bksp	14	| or \	43	Num Lock	69
Tab	15	Z	44	Scroll Lock	70
Q	16	X	45	Home or 7	71
W	17	C	46	Up or 8	72
E	18	V	47	PgUp or 9	73
R	19	B	48	Grey -	74
T	20	N	49	Left or 4	75
Y	21	M	50	Centre or 5	76
U	22	< or ,	51	Right or 6	77
I	23	> or .	52	Grey +	78
O	24	? or /	53	End or 1	79
P	25	Right Shift	54	Down or 2	80
{ or [	26	Prt Sc or *	55	PgDn or 3	81
} or]	27	Alt	56	Ins or 0	82
Enter	28	Spacebar	57	Del or .	83
Ctrl	29				

Table ON KEY #1

ON PEN

Type:	Statement
Typical syntax:	ON PEN GOSUB line
Action:	Provides a routine to use when a light-pen event is trapped, meaning that following PEN ON, the light-pen is moved.
Options:	None.
Argument(s):	None.
Restrictions:	The light-pen must be connected and trapping of the event must be enabled by using PEN ON.

Example:

```
ON PEN GOSUB penprint        'name routine
PEN ON                       'start trapping
REM Try moving pen
PRINT "Press any key to end trapping"
DO WHILE INKEY$ = ""
LOOP
penprint:
FOR j% = 1 TO 9
  PRINT "Pen code ";j%; " is ";PEN(j%)
NEXT
RETURN
```

Associated with: ON, OFF, PEN, STOP

Points to note:
None.

ON PLAY

Type:	Statement
Typical syntax:	ON PLAY (queuesize) GOSUB line
Action:	Provides a routine to use when a play event is trapped – usually this provides for repeating the music string when the buffer is empty or almost empty.
Options:	None.
Argument(s):	The length of the music queue (integer 1 to 31) that is to trigger the action, enclosed in brackets. The branch will occur if the number of notes in the buffer is less than this specified number.
Restrictions:	Trappings of event must have been enabled by using PLAY ON. The argument must not be zero.

Example:

```
PLAY ON                          'activate trapping
ON PLAY(5) GOSUB playit          'set trap
M$="t9Oo3L4cco2b8o2a.GFfe8f8g4d2e2L6f#"
N$="ga.O3d2o2L4go3ccc16O2b.A8g4"
Tune$                            'define notes
PLAY Tune$                       'start playing
PRINT "Press any key to stop"    'can't do this
DO WHILE INKEY$ = ""             'at the Proms
LOOP
END
playit:                          'trap routine
PRINT" Play it again, Sam"
PLAY Tune$                       'plays it again
RETURN
REM lowercase o and uppercase L used to avoid
REM confusion with O and 1.
```

Associated with: OFF, ON, PLAY function, PLAY statement, STOP

Points to note:

When the action is triggered it does not cause the tune to be suddenly restarted. The restart will occur only when the current tune has ended, so that any argument from 1 to 31 is effective if the tune has more than 31 notes. The restart is not so abrupt if the tune starts with a rest of short duration.

ON STRIG

Type: Statement

Typical syntax: ON STRIG (number) GOSUB line

Action: Provides a routine to use when a joystick trigger is pressed.

Options: None.

Argument(s):   The integer argument determines which joystick trigger is used, enclosed in brackets.

0	Lower trigger,	joystick A
2	Lower trigger,	joystick B
4	Upper trigger,	joystick A
6	Upper trigger,	joystick B

Restrictions: One or two joysticks must be connected and trapping of the event must have been enabled by using STRIG ON.

Example:

```
STRIG (0) ON
STRIG (2) ON
ON STRIG (0) GOSUB zerotrig
ON STRIG (2) GOSUB twotrig
PRINT "Press any key to stop"
DO WHILE INKEY$ = ""
LOOP
zerotrig:
LOCATE 10,10
PRINT "Trigger 0"
RETURN
twotrig:
LOCATE 20,20
PRINT "Trigger 2"
RETURN
```

Associated with: OFF, ON, STICK, STRIG function, STOP

Points to note:

When a STRIG event is trapped, the routine is stopped to prevent it from calling itself. Event trapping is re-enabled by the RETURN statement unless the STRIG subroutine has included a STRIG OFF line.

ON TIMER

Type:	Statement
Typical syntax:	ON TIMER (number) GOSUB line
Action:	Provides a routine which is activated at regular intervals as determined by the argument. Typically used to print a time on the screen which will be updated each second or each minute.
Options:	None.
Argument(s):	The number of seconds that pass before the branch to the event-trapping subroutine, enclosed in brackets. This can be in the range 1 to 86,400 (24 hours).
Restrictions:	Trapping of the event must have been enabled by using TIMER ON.

Example:

```
CLS
ON TIMER (10) GOSUB looktime    'set up routine, 10 seconds
TIMER ON                        'activate
PRINT
FOR n% = 1 TO 100               'slow loop which will
   PRINT "Count is "; n%         'run while timer
   FOR j = 1 TO 3000: NEXT       'works
NEXT
END

looktime                        'timer routine
col % = POS (0)                 'save the cursor col
row% = CSRLIN                   'and row positions
LOCATE 1, 70                    'place for time print
PRINT TIME$                     'print it here
LOCATE row%, col%               'cursor back in place
RETURN                          'back to work
```

Associated with: OFF, ON, TIMER, TIME$ function, STOP

Points to note:

When the subroutine called by the TIMER trap runs, further timer interrupts are turned off until the RETURN statement is met. Using a TIMER OFF statement in the subroutine will prevent the timer trapping from being resumed after the first call.

OPEN

Type:	Statement
Typical syntax:	OPEN filename AS filenumber
	OPEN filename FOR mode AS filenumber
	OPEN filename ACCESS type AS filenumber
Action:	Opens a file or device for reading or writing or both, using a reference number, often referred to as a *file handle*. The type of file determines what size of unit (from a byte to a complete file) is read or written. Networking statements allow for restriction of file access where required. The record size for random-access record, (512 bytes for the serial buffer).
Options:	A networking lock option can use the words SHARED, LOCK READ, LOCK WRITE, LOCK READWRITE. The LEN=length option can be used for a random-access file to specify the length of each record or, for a sequential file, the buffer size.
Argument(s):	The filename can include a full path along with the filename if needed. The filenumber can use 1 to 255, and can optionally be preceded by the hash sign, such as #2. Using the hash is a good way of identifying a filenumber and distinguishing it from other numbers.

The mode option can use :

APPEN	–	allowing data to be added to the end of a sequential file
BINARY	–	storing data one byte at a time with access to each byte
INPUT	–	allowing writing to a sequential file (replacing existing file information)
OUTPUT	–	allowing reading of a sequential file
RANDOM	–	opening a random-access file for reading or writing.

The ACCESS type is intended for networking only, allowing you to specify READ, WRITE or READWRITE.

Restrictions:	Use an ACCESS type only when a network is involved.

Examples:

(a) Sequential file

```
DECLARE SUB fields (rc$)              'procedure
CLS
OPEN "aircraft.dat" FOR APPEND AS #5  'will create if new
rc$ = ""                             'clear variable
DIM SHARED x AS INTEGER               'x is global counter
PRINT TAB(27); "DATA ENTRY": PRINT    'heading
DO WHILE UCASE$(rc$) <> "X"           'main loop
PRINT
INPUT "Name of this record "; rc$     'ask for name
IF UCASE$(rc$) <> "X" THEN CALL fields(rc$)  'send to file
LOOP                                  'end of loop
PRINT x; " records on file ."         'count report
CLOSE                                 'close file
END
DATA Country of origin,Type,Engines,Empty weight (kg),
DATA Accommodation

SUB fields (recordname$)              'file procedure
PRINT #5, recordname$: x = x + 1      'print to file
RESTORE                               'restore data
FOR n% = 1 TO 5                       'get the
READ head$                            'headings for
PRINT head$; " ";: INPUT field$       'entries, and input
PRINT #5, field$                      'print to file
NEXT                                  'and again
END SUB                               'until 5 done
REM The optional # sign has been used in OPEN and PRINT
lines
REM This can be used to update file also because
REM APPEND has been used rather than OPEN.
```

(b) Random-access file recording

```
CLS
ON ERROR GOTO getout
REM close file on error such as request for record zero
```

```
FILE% =1: LIMIT% =100              'set numbers
DIM A AS INTEGER                   'A is integer for filing
OPEN "integer.rnd" FOR RANDOM AS #FILE% LEN = 2    'open
FOR n% = 1 TO LIMIT%              'loop for entry
INPUT A                           'get integer from keyboard
PUT FILE%, n%, A                  'put in file
NEXT                              'back for another
getout:                           'emergency exit
CLOSE                             'close files
END
REM Gets integer numbers from keyboard and places in
REM a random access file #1.
REM Note modern system, not using FIELD, RSET, LSET, MKI$,
CVI
```

Associated with: CLOSE, FREEFILE, OPEN COM, TYPE

Points to note:

A device can be opened, allowing for instance PRN, COM or CON to be allocated with a filenumber and written to as if a file. The COM and CON devices can also be read. For example:

```
OPEN "PRN:" FOR OUTPUT AS #6
```

will allow the use of PRINT #6 to send text to the printer. There is an alternative syntax for OPEN which is intended for compatibility with older versions of BASIC and which should not now be used in programming.

The old syntax is:

```
OPEN ch$, #number, filename$
OPEN ch$, #number, filename$, length
```

and typical examples are:

```
OPEN "O", #1, "C\DATA\AIRCRAFT.DAT", 48
OPEN "R", #2, "C\DATA\RANDFIL.RND"
```

In which the letters used as ch$ are:

A	Append to sequential file.
B	Binary file.
I	Input from sequential file.
O	Output to new sequential file.
R	Random access read or write.

The other portions of the statement are the file handle number, which is of the same form as the later OPEN statement, the file name, and the record length number. For sequential files, the length number will determine the size of the buffer used for the sequential files.

If you come across an old program using this method, it can be run on QBASIC, but it is better to convert any program that you intend to use more than once. Any attempt to open a nonexistent file for reading will produce the *File not found* error, number 53. Trying to open a non-existent file for OUTPUT, APPEND, BINARY or RANDOM will *not* cause an error – the file will be created instead provided the filename is a valid one.

OPEN COM

Type: Statement

Typical syntax: OPEN "COM1: mainoption minoroption" AS number

OPEN "COM2: mainoption minoroption" FOR mode AS number

Action: Opens a specified serial port, sets serial parameters and specifies the use for the port.

Options: LEN=length can be appended to specify the number of bytes used for the buffer, default 128 bytes. The number can use 1 to 255 with or without a preceding hash. The mode can be INPUT, OUTPUT or RANDOM.

Argument(s): The mainoption set contains the parameters that are most often needed for communications use. These are baud rate, parity, data length and number of stop bits.

The permitted baud rates are 75, 110, 150, 300, 600, 1200, 2400, 4800 or 9600.

The parity is N (none) E (even) O (odd) S (space) M (mark) or PE (enable parity error checking)

The data length is the number of data bits per byte: 5, 6, 7, or 8

The number of stop bits is 1, 1.5 or 2

The defaults are 300 baud, even parity, 7 data bits, 1 stop bit.

The minoroption set contains parameters which are very seldom needed. These are:

ASC	Opens the port to use in ASCII mode
BIN	Opens the port to use in binary mode.
CDtime	Sets a timeout period (in Milliseconds) on the Data Carrier Detect (DCD) line.
CStime	Sets a timeout period (in milliseconds) on the Clear to Send (CTS) line.
DStime	Sets a timeout period (in milliseconds) on the Data Set Ready (DSR) line.
LF	Sends a line-feed character after a carriage return.
OPtime	Specifies how long (in milliseconds) OPEN COM waits for all communications lines to become open.

RBsize   Sets the size (in bytes) of the receive buffer.

RS   Suppresses detection of Request to Send (RTS).

TBsize   Sets the size (in bytes) of the transmit buffer.

Note that word such as *time* and *size* indicate that a number is to follow the command option letters.

Restrictions: The serial port cannot be used by QBASIC to read or write data unless this form of OPEN statement has been used, but an event can be detected.

Examples:

(a)

```
COM (2) ON                'My COM1 is used by mouse
ON COM (2) GOSUB readport 'routine for COM2
PRINT "Press any key to stop" 'how to escape
DO WHILE INKEY$ = " "     'start loop
LOOP                      'until event or key pressed
COM(2) OFF                'end trapping

readport:                 'detect
PRINT "Message received"  'character at port
RETURN                    'but do not read it
```

(b)   Prints received file

```
ON COM(2) GOSUB getinput  'use COM2
COM(2) ON                 'activate
OPEN "com2:" FOR RANDOM AS #1 'open using defaults
DO WHILE INKEY$ = " "     'infinite
PRINT combuf$             'loop
LOOP                      'until key or message
END

getinput:                 'COM routine
INUT #1,combuf$           'get a line
RETURN                    'that's all
REM Do not confuse use of #1, file handle number
REM with use of 2 as COM port number.
```

Associated with: OPEN, COM, ON COM

Points to note:

The default baud rate is 300, which by modern standards is painfully slow. A rate of 2400 is more appropriate.

OPTION

Type: Statement

Typical syntax: OPTION BASE number

Action: Allows the first element of an array to use subscript 0
                     or 1.

Options: None.

Argument (s):   Number is 0 or 1.

Restrictions: Used only along with BASE.

Example:

```
DIM X% (50)       'subscripts 0 to 50 can be used
OPTION BASE (1)
DIM A$(50)        'subscripts 1 to 50 can be used
```

Associated with: DIM, REDIM, LBOUND, UBOUND

Points to note:

A better method is to use the DIM statement with its TO clause, for
example:

```
DIM A$ (2 TO 50)
```

This allows numbers other than 0 or 1 to be used.

OR

Type:	Operator returning Boolean TRUE or FALSE
Typical syntax:	(expression1) OR (expression2)
Action:	Returns TRUE if either or both expressions return TRUE. As a table this is:

Expression1	Expression2	Result
FALSE	FALSE	FALSE
FALSE	TRUE	TRUE
TRUE	FALSE	TRUE
TRUE	TRUE	TRUE

Options:	None.
Argument(s):	Two Boolean expressions, one on each side of the OR operator.
Restrictions:	Each expression must be capable of being resolved as TRUE or FALSE. The precedence is low, following arithmetic and relational operations. OR should not be used with numbers because its bitwise action can produce unexpected results.

Example:

```
IF (Age = 55) OR (Name = "XX") THEN EXIT DO
REM Either or both will break loop
```

Associated with: AND, EXP, IMP, NOT, XOR

Points to note:

Use with numbers can produce confusing results because each bit of the binary form of one number is ORed with the corresponding bit of the other number. For example, 6 OR 14 is 14 because in binary this is 0110 OR 1110, giving 1110.

The OR action is sometimes called *disjunction* or *inclusive OR*.

OUT

Type:	Statement
Typical syntax:	OUT port, data
Action:	Send out a single byte at the specified port address.
Options:	None.
Argument(s):	Address number of port, single byte of data to send out.
Restrictions:	Only one byte at a time can be sent.

Example:

```
LS% = INP(&H61)        'read status register
LS% = LS% AND &HOOFC   'use 0000000011111100 for mask
FOR j% = 1 TO 800      'loop for loudspeaker note
LS% = LS% XOR 2        'reverse bit 1
OUT &H61, LS%          'put out
FOR X%=1 TO 5:NEXT     'brief wait
NEXT                   'then again
END
REM causes sound by switching the loudspeaker on
REM and off rapidly in a loop
```

Associated with: INP, WAIT

Points to note:

This is another command which requires a knowledge of machine-code programming and the design of the PC machine. You need to know the port address numbers and the effect of sending a byte from the port.

OUTPUT

Type:	Statement
Typical syntax:	Open filename FOR OUTPUT AS number
Option:	None.
Argument(s):	None.
Restrictions:	Used only along wih OPEN statement.
Action:	Opens a sequential file for output, replacing any previous file of the same name.

Example:

```
OPEN "Myfile. SER" FOR OUTPUT AS #2
REM Opens new file, replacing any old one
REM of the same name
REM use APPEND otherwise
```

Associated with: APPEND, BINARY, INPUT, OPEN, RANDOM

Points to note:

Use APPEND to add data to a sequential file. APPEND will also create and open a new file if no file of the specified name exists, so that APPEND is to be preferred unless you specifically want a new file to replace an old one of the same name.

PAINT

Type:	Statement
Typical syntax:	PAINT (position)
	PAINT (position), colour
	PAINT (position), tilepattern
	PAINT (position), colour, border
	PAINT (position), colour, border, background
Action:	Fills a closed area with a specified colour and/or pattern. The area is filled up to a specified boundary.
Options:	Either a colour number (an integer) or a tilepattern string can be placed following the position co-ordinates. The border colour and background colour numbers can also be added, following commas, to the main statement. A STEP option, placed ahead of the position co-ordinates, allows the position co-ordinates to be taken as relative to the current cursor position.
Argument(s):	Co-ordinates to specify position to start filling with paint colour, colour number for filling area. The tile option allows a pattern to be defined using one string character for each eight bits of the pattern. Typically this would use a statement such as:

```
fill$ = CHR$(byte1) + CHR$(byte2) +
… up to 64 bytes.
```

The border colour number specifies the colour of the border which is used as the boundary where the filling action will stop.

The background colour number allows you to paint over an area that has already been painted.

Restrictions:	The type of graphics card used and the most-recently used SCREEN statement will affect the PAINT action.
Example:	

```
SCREEN 12                    'VGA being used
COLOR 0                      'foreground text colour
CIRCLE (320, 240), 88, 14    'draw yellow circle
CIRCLE (320, 240), 30, 14    'and another
PAINT (350, 290), 5, 14      'paint between them
```

Associated with: #DRAW, SCREEN

Points to note:

Any opening in the boundary will allow colour to leak and fill the whole screen. The starting point for PAINT must be within the area that is to be filled, not on the border.

PALETTE

Type:	Statement
Typical syntax:	PALETTE
	PALETTE attrib,column
	PALETTE USING array
	PALETTE USING array(index)
Action:	Changes the colours assigned to the attribute numbers for the screen mode being used.
Options:	The USING option allows you to specify the name of an array that contains colour values that can be assigned to the attributes for the screen mode that is currently in use. This array must be large enough to assign colours to all of the attributes that can be used. You can also specify the subscript number (index) of the first array element to assign to an attribute.
Argument(s):	Optionally, the colour attribute number to change and a colour value to assign to an attribute.
Restrictions:	This statement can be used on EGA, VGA and MCGA screens only, not CGA or Hercules.

Example:

```
SCREEN 12                          'use VGA
PALETTE                            'default
LINE (10,10) 600,400), 1, BF      'draw filled box
DO                                 'loop
  FOR j% = 2 TO 14                 'using these numbers
    PALETTE 1, j %                 'change palette
    SLEEP .5                       'wait
  NEXT                             'next one
LOOP WHILE INKEY$ = ""             'hold down key to stop
END
```

Associated with: COLOR, SCREEN

Points to note:

See SCREEN entry for details of colour numbers.

PALETTE USING requires an array to be dimensioned as an integer with sufficient subscripts to allow for the range of colour numbers you will be using. Each subscript number in the array is used as a palette number for whatever colour number is present in the array at that subscript number. An entry of -1 as a colour number is permitted, and is used to mean no change in the attribute; no other negative number is permitted. For example:

```
PALETTE 0, 1                        'Starting set
SCREEN 9                            'VGA or EGA
Dim a % (15)                        'array
FOR i% = 0 TO 15                    'fill with
a%(i%) = i%                         'integers
NEXT
LINE (200, 20)-(300, 100), 3, BF   'draw box
LINE (20, 20)-(200, 140), 2, BF    'and another
DO WHILE INKEY$ = ""                'start loop
  FOR i% = 0 TO 15                  'and another
      a%(i%) = (a%(i%) + 1) MOD 16 'to cycle numbers
  NEXT i%                           'all one up
  PALETTE USING a%(0)              'and use them
  SLEEP 1                           'wait to see
LOOP                                'next set
```

In this example, which cycles the numbers held in the array, the SLEEP line gives time for viewing, and the display can be speeded up by removing this line.

PCOPY

Type:	Statement
Typical syntax:	PCOPY source destination
Action:	Copies the contents of one numbered video page to another specified page number.
Options:	None.
Argument(s):	Numbers for source and destination video pages.
Restrictions:	Can be used only when multiple video pages are enabled – which depends on the graphics mode currently in use.

Example:

```
SCREEN 8                        'allows several pages
CIRCLE (320, 100), 50, 4        'draw this
PCOPY 0, 1                      'copy to 1
CIRCLE (320, 100), 100, 5       'draw this
PCOPY 0, 2                      'copy to 2
CIRCLE (320, 100), 150, 6       'draw this
PCOPY 0, 3                      'copy to 3
CLS                             'clear 0
FOR n% = 1 TO 3                 'start loop
  PCOPY n%, 0                   'copy screen pattern
  SLEEP 1                       'wait
NEXT                            'then another
```

Associated with: SCREEN

Points to note:

PCOPY is useful mainly on the low-resolution screens, because the high-resolution screens do not permit the use of multiple pages. On a low-resolution screen, PCOPY can be used as a way of animating drawings.

PEEK

Type:	Function returning integer
Typical syntax:	PEEK (address)
Action:	Returns the byte stored at the specified address.
Options:	None.
Argument(s):	The address number, placed within brackets, must be in the range 0 to 65536 (hex &H0000 to &HFFFF).
Restrictions:	The address that is used will be in the current memory segment. Use DEF SEG to change segment if necessary.

Example:

```
CLS
a% = 293                    'assign integer
x% = VARPTR(a%)             'get its address as x%
FOR n% = 0 TO 1            'read both of
  PRINT PEEK(x% + n%)      'the bytes here and following
NEXT                        'which are 37 and 1
REM Because one byte can store 256 digits, this number
REM is 1 x 256 + 37 = 293. The higher order (number
REM of 256s) is stored following the lower order (units)
```

Associated with: DEF SEG, POKE, VARPTR, VARPTR$

Points to note:

PEEK should be used only by programmers with a good understanding of machine-code and a thorough understanding of the memory structure of the PC machine.

PEN function

Type: Function returning integer

Typical syntax: variable = PEN(number)

Action: Returns with information about the light-pen.

Options: None.

Argument(s):   The number argument, placed within brackets, determines what the PEN function will return, as shown in Table PEN #1.

number	quantity returned
0	Whether pen was used since last call (-1 if yes, 0 if no).
1	The x screen coordinate of the last pen press.
2	The y screen coordinate of the last pen press.
3	The current pen switch status (-1 if down, 0 if up).
4	The x screen coordinate where the pen last left the screen.
5	The y screen coordinate where the pen last left the screen.
6	The character row of the last pen press.
7	The character column of the last pen press.
8	The character row where the pen last left the screen.
9	The character column where the pen last left the screen.

Table PEN #1. PEN function number arguments.

Restrictions: Useable only if the appropriate hardware is installed. Very few computers are equipped with a light-pen socket.

Example:

```
ON PEN GOSUB penprint           'name routine
PEN ON                          'start trapping
REM Try moving pen
PRINT "Press any key to end trapping"
DO WHILE INKEY$ = ""
LOOP
penprint:
FOR j% = 1 TO 9                             'set of codes
PRINT "Pen code ";j%; " is ";PEN(j%)    'print values
NEXT
RETURN
```

Associated with: PEN, ON PEN, SCREEN

Points to note:

Light pens used on the PC are comparatively rare, so that you are not likely to make use of this function.

PEN statement

Type:	Statement
Typical syntax:	PEN ON
	PEN OFF
	PEN STOP
	ON PEN GOSUB line
Action:	PEN ON Enables, PEN OFF disables and PEN STOP suspends pen event trapping action. ON PEN GOSUB provides the line label name or number for the routine that runs when a PEN event, if enabled, occurs.
Options:	None.
Argument(s):	ON enables PEN event trapping, OFF disables. STOP suspends trapping, so that if an event occurs it is not acted on until the PEN ON statement is used. The ON PEN GOSUB statement requires a line label or number for the routine that will be run when a pen event occurs.
Restrictions:	Pen hardware must be installed.
Example:	See PEN function example.
Associated with:	ON, OFF, PEN function, STOP

Points to note:

As above – the use of light pens on PC machines is rare.

PLAY function

Type: Function returning integer.

Typical syntax: variable = PLAY(number)

Action: Returns the number of notes waiting in the PLAY queue (0 to 31).

Options: None.

Argument(s):   The number argument, between brackets, is a dummy and the value is not used. It must nevertheless be provided.

Restrictions: PLAY returns only the number of notes in the background buffer. If the music is not playing or is in the foreground (nothing else running) PLAY returns zero.

Example:

```
A$ = "O3CDEFGABO4C"          'define play string
PLAY A$                      'start playing
DO                           'loop
  j% = PLAY(1)               'find how many left
   PRINT j%; " notes remaining"  'and print it
LOOP UNTIL j% = 0            'and again…
END
```

Associated with: ON PLAY, PLAY

Points to note:

Used to check when another PLAY statement can be used without needing to wait for the sound buffer to be emptied.

PLAY statement(1)

Type:	Statement
Typical syntax:	PLAY ON
	PLAY OFF
	PLAY STOP
	ON PLAY(queuelimit%) GOSUB line
Action:	Provides for a routine to use when a play event is trapped – usually this provides for repeating the music string when the buffer is empty or almost empty. PLAY ON enables the PLAY trapping; PLAY OFF disables the action. Using PLAY STOP will suspend trapping, but if an event occurs while PLAY STOP is effective, the trapping will be done when a PLAY ON is encountered.
	For details of ON PLAY, see under that heading.
Options:	None.
Argument(s):	ON enables trapping, OFF disables, and STOP suspends, see Action above.
Restrictions:	This form of PLAY statement uses ON, OFF, STOP only. See the following entry for PLAY string statement.

Example:

```
PLAY ON                              'activate trapping
ON PLAY(5) GOSUB playit              'set trap
M$="T9003L4CC02B803C8D02A.G.FFE8F8G4D2E2L6F#"
N$ = "GA.03D202L4G03CCC1602B.A8G4"
Tune$ = M$ + N$                      'define notes
PLAY Tune$                           'start playing
Print "Press any key to stop"        'can't do this
DO WHILE INKEY$ = ""                 'at the proms
LOOP
END
playit:                              'trap routine
PRINT" Play it, Sam"
PLAY Tune$                           'play it again
RETURN
```

Associated with: PLAY music statement, ON PLAY

Points to note:

This form of PLAY statemen is associated with PLAY event trappping. For the normal playing of music, use the PLAY string statement following.

PLAY statement(2)

Type: Statement

Typical syntax: PLAY musicstring

Action: Plays notes as commanded by letters and numbers in a string.

Options: None.

Argument(s): The argument is a string of instructions using the following letters and numbers:

A - G	Play musical note A to G.
# or +	Sharpen note by a semitone (placed following letter).
-	Flatten note by one semitone (placed following letter).
.	Increase duration of note by 50%.
<	Move down one octave.
>	Move up one octave .
Lnumber	Set length, number 1 to 64, 0 for a rest. L4 is a crochet.
MB	Play music in background.
MF	Play music in foreground.
ML	Set style legato.
MN	Set style normal.
MS	Set style staccato.
Nnumber	Play specified note (0 to 84) in a 7-octave range. This is an alternative to selecting octave and note letter.
Onumber	Sets the current octave (numbers 0 - 6).
Pnumber	Specifies a pause (numbers 1 - 64). P4 is a crochet pause.
Tnumber	Sets the tempo in quarter notes per minute (32 - 255).
X	Execute subroutine string (see Restrictions).

Restrictions: Following X, a sub-string must use VARPTR$ in the form:

```
"X" + VARPTR$(X$)
```

Examples:

(a)
```
A$ = "T120L403CDEFL16GABO4L2C" 'string to play
PLAY A$:'hear how it sounds    'normal
PLAY "MN" + A$: 'Normal        'also normal
PLAY "MS" + A$: 'Staccato      'short bursts
PLAY "ML" + A$: 'Legato        'smoothly flowing
```

(b)
```
CLS
DO
PRINT "What tempo would you like (1 to 255. 0 to end) ";
INPUT TEMPO%                      'set timing
IF TEMPO% = 0 THEN END            'get out
PRINT "playing....": GOSUB playit 'subroutine
LOOP
END

playit:
M$ ="O3L4CCO2B803C8DO2A.G.FFE8F8G4D2E2L6F#"
N$ = "GA.03D202L4G03CCC1602B.A8G4"
M$ = M$ + N$              'full music string
PLAY "T=" + VARPTR$(TEMPO%) + M$ 'add tempo with VARPTRS
RETURN
```

Associated with: BEEP, PLAY function, ON PLAY action, SOUND,
                       VARPTR$

Points to note:

The PLAY string allows a large range of commands over the note pitch,
octave, tempo, style etc.

PMAP

Type:	Function returning integer or long-integer number
Typical syntax:	PMAP (start, number)
Action:	Converts a co-ordinate value after the WINDOW statement has been used to change the co-ordinates used by the screen. For example, the normal range of X = 0 to 639 and Y = 0 to 479 can be changed, using WINDOW to X = 0 to 1000 and Y = 0 to 1000. PMAP is then used to translate from a value in one co-ordinate set to the correct value in the other.
Options:	None.
Argument(s):	The first argument is a co-ordinate, X or Y which can be an ordinary full-screen co-ordinate in the range 0-639, 0-479 or one for a new co-ordinate set that has been put in place by a WINDOW statement. The second argument determines which conversion is used:

0	converts	Normal	x	coordinate	to	Window x coordinate
1	converts	Normal	y	coordinate	to	Window y coordinate
2	converts	Window	x	coordinate	to	Normal x coordinate
3	converts	Window	y	coordinate	to	Normal y coordinate

Restrictions:	PMAP cannot be used unless WINDOW has previously been used.
Example:	

```
SCREEN 12                          'VGA
WINDOW (0,0) - (1000,1000)         'new co-ordinates
PSET (PMAP(5,0), PMAP(10,1))       'set a point, old
PSET (PMAP(900,2), PMAP(900,3))    'and another, new
PRINT PMAP(5,0)                    'print
PRINT PMAP(10,1)                   'the values
PRINT PMAP(600,2)                  'that have
PRINT PMAP(400,3)                  'been used
```

Associated with: POINT, VIEW, WINDOW

Points to note:

It is only too easy to mix up the actions, so that variables such as oldX, oldY, newX and newY can be helpful for storing co-ordinate values.

POINT

Type:	Function returning integer
Typical syntax:	POINT (number)
	POINT (coordinates)
Action:	When used with a single number, returns one co-ordinate of the present position of the graphics cursor using either the normal co-ordinates (0-639 and 0-479 for VGA) or whatever co-ordinates have been assigned using a WINDOW statement. When used with a pair of co-ordinates, POINT returns the colour of the pixel at that point (-1 if the point is outside the current viewing window).
Options:	A single number argument or pair of co-ordinates.
Argument(s):	When used with a single number:

0	The current normal screen x co-ordinate.
1	The current normal screen y coordinate.
2	The current x coordinate as changed by WINDOW.
3	The current y coordinate as changed by WINDOW.

Otherwise uses a pair of co-ordinates enclosed in brackets and separated by a comma.

Restrictions:	The co-ordinates used must correspond to an actual point.

Example:

```
(a)  SCREEN 12                 'VGA
     CIRCLE (320, 240), 200,2  'large circle
     PSET (320, 240),1         'point at centre
     PRINT POINT (320,240)     'gives 1 as colour number
     PRINT POINT(0), POINT(1)  'gives co-ordinates
(b)  SCREEN 12                 'VGA
     COLOR 0
     CLS
     FOR Y% = 0 TO 199         'draw one vertical
       PSET (10, Y%), 14       'line down screen
     NEXT
     FOR Y% = 0 TO 199         'and now another
```

```
      PSET (254, Y%), 14
NEXT
K% = 1: x% = 11: Y% = 1      'initial position numbers
DO WHILE Y% < 199           'for Y-range
   PSET (x%, Y%), 14         'place dot
IF POINT(x% + K%, Y%) <> 0 THEN      'if at boundary
   K% = -K%                  'reverse X movement
   Y% = Y% + 1              'and step downwards
END IF
FOR x = 1 TO 10: NEXT       'short delay
PRESET (x%, Y%)             'wipe out dot
x% = x% + K%ihh*i           'increment position
LOOP 'and again
```

Associated with: COLOR, PMAP, SCREEN, VIEW, WINDOW

Points to note:

POINT is a valuable function for use in animation and in tracing a path through a maze.

POKE

Type:	Statement
Typical syntax:	POKE address, value
Action:	Alters the content of a memory address by placing a specified value at that address.
Options:	None.
Argument(s):	The address in the current segment (see Appendix C) and the value to poke, separated by a comma.
Restrictions:	Unless DEF SEG is used to change the segment, the POKE action will affect addresses in the current segment. Address numbers are restricted to the range 0 to 65535.

Example:

```
CLS
a$ = "This is a string"               'assign string
x% = VARPTR(a$)                        'find pointer
a% = PEEK(x% + 2) + 256 * (PEEK(x% + 3)) 'find address
FOR n% = 0 TO 15                       'in loop
   POKE a% + n%, 65                    'change letter to A
   PRINT a$                           'print result
NEXT                                   'as loop progresses
```

Associated with: DEF SEG, PEEK, VARPTR, VARPTR$, VARSEG

Points to note:

This is a statement which should be used only by experienced machine-code programmers, since it allows the memory to be altered at will. Badly-placed POKE statements could wipe out data in the memory, causing the machine to lock up, for which the only cure is a reboot. If you have a BASIC program that contains POKE statements, make sure that you have the file saved before attempting to run it.

Be careful of POKE statements if you are converting programs written in another variety of BASIC. BASIC is a high-level language, which means that a program written in BASIC can often be run on a variety of machines. If a BASIC program contains a POKE statement, however, it makes that program specific to a machine and sometimes to one version of BASIC.

POS

Type:	Function returning integer number
Typical syntax:	POS(dummy number)
Action:	Returns the current column number for the text cursor.
Options:	None.
Argument(s):	Any number or expression; a dummy value, enclosed in brackets.
Restrictions:	Operates on the text screen only.

Example:

```
CLS
LOCATE 5, 4                 'first position
A$ = "HERE"                 'first string
GOSUB slowprint             'print slowly
col% = POS(1)               'store col position
row% = CSRLIN               'and row
LOCATE 20, 5                'new position
A$ = "THERE"                'new string
GOSUB slowprint             'print slowly
LOCATE row%, col%           'back to place
A$ = "AGAIN"                'another string
GOSUB slowprint             'print it slowly
END                         'that's it.
slowprint:
FOR j% = 1 TO LEN(A$)       'letter by letter
   PRINT MID$(A$, j%, 1);   'select and print
   SLEEP 1                  'delay (too fast otherwise)
NEXT                        'then next
PRINT " ";                  'put in space
RETURN                      'return
```

Associated with: CSRLIN, LOCATE, VIEW PRINT

Points to note:

The normal use of POS along with CSRLIN is, as indicated in the example, to store a cursor position so that it can be used later. This is particularly important if printing is being done in several screen windows.

PRESET

Type:	Statement
Typical syntax:	PRESET (coordinates)
	PRESET (coordinates), colour
Action:	Resets the colour of a specified pixel to the current background colour or to a specified new background colour.
Options:	STEP placed ahead of coordinates makes all co-ordinate numbers relative to current cursor position. The colour number is also optional, and PRESET is normally used to make a pixel invisible after it has been made visible using PSET.
Argument(s):	The co-ordinates, within brackets, are for a pixel on the graphics screen. A colour number can be used to reset the pixel colour to this other colour. Normally, PSET and PRESET are used with no colour arguments.
Restrictions:	Any colour number that is used must be valid for the type of SCREEN mode being used.

Example:

```
SCREEN 12                        'VGA
COLOR 0
CLS
FOR Y% = 0 TO 199                'draw one vertical
   PSET (10, Y%), 14             'line down screen
NEXT
FOR Y% = 0 TO 199                'and now another
   PSET (254, Y%), 14
NEXT
K% = 1: x% = 11: Y% = 1          'initial position numbers
DO WHILE Y% < 199                'for Y-range
   PSET (x%, Y%), 14             'place dot
   IF POINT(x% + K%, Y%) <> 0 THEN      'if at boundary
     K% = -K%                    'reverse X movement
     Y% = Y% + 1                 'and step downwards
   END IF
```

```
    FOR x = 1 TO 10: NEXT        'short delay
    PRESET (x%, Y%)              'wipe out dot
    x% = x% + K%                 'increment position
 LOOP 'and again
```

Associated with: PSET, SCREEN, VIEW, WINDOW

Points to note:

PSET and PRESET together form a way of creating images one pixel at a
time. This is slow, and should be used only for a fairly small number of
pixels, or for purposes where speed is not important. For elaborate
drawings, use the DRAW statement.

PRINT

Type:	Statement
Typical syntax:	PRINT variablename
	PRINT #number, variablename
Action:	Prints text on screen or in a selected window (viewport). Can also be used along with a file number to print to a file or device.
Options:	A list of variables can be printed. If the items are separated by semicolons they are run on, if they are separated by commas each new item will start in a new print zone, using zones 14 characters apart.
	See also PRINT USING.
Argument(s):	Any number or string variable or literal. A literal string must be enclosed in quotes.
Restrictions:	The PRINT #2 type of output requires a file of this number to be open. A semicolon is used to separate a literal (in quotes) from a variable item.

Examples:

(a)
```
a% = 5                  'assign number
PRINT "Number"; a%      'print literal and variable
FOR X% = 1 TO 5         'print set
PRINT X%,               'of numbers in zones
NEXT
FOR X% = 1 TO 5         'print set of numbers
PRINT X%;               'packed together
PRINT "ONE ";
PRINT "TWO"             'together on line
```

(b)
```
DECLARE SUB fields (rc$)
CLS
OPEN "aircraft.dat" FOR APPEND AS #5   'open file
rc$ = ""                               'initialise
DIM SHARED x AS INTEGER                'declare
PRINT TAB(27); "DATA ENTRY"            'heading
PRINT
DO WHILE UCASE$(rc$) <> "X"            'loop
```

```
PRINT
INPUT "Name of this record "; rc$        'type name
IF UCASE$(rc$) <> "X" THEN CALL fields(rc$) 'record
LOOP                                     'end of record
PRINT x; " records on file ."            'end of file
CLOSE                                    'close file
END

DATA Country of origin,Type,Engines,     'headings
DATA Empty weight (kg),Accommodation

SUB fields (recordname$)                 'record entry
PRINT #5, recordname$                    'print to file
x = x + 1                               'increment counter
RESTORE                                  'headings
FOR n% = 1 TO 5                          'to read in
READ head$
PRINT head$; " ";                        'and use
INPUT field$                             'as prompts
PRINT #5, field$                         'put to file
NEXT                                     'and again
END SUB                                  'go back
```

Associated with: LPRINT, OPEN, WIDTH, WRITE

Points to note:

WRITE is more often used in the form WRITE #5 to write to a file.

PRINT USING

Type:	Statement
Typical syntax:	PRINT USING formatstring, variablename
	PRINT USING #number, formatstring, variablename
Action:	Prints numbers and strings each arranged in a field space and conforming to a pattern set by a string of markers.
Options:	The semicolon and comma modifiers can be used in a list of items to be printed with the same effect as in a PRINT statement, see earlier.
Argument(s):	The formatting string consists of characters that determine how the numbers or characters of the printed material will be arranged.
String fields:	Backslash characters are used as markers to define the size of a field to contain a string – the size of the field is the size of the space defined by the backslashes and the spaces between them. For example:

`"\    \"`

contains six spaces, making a total field width of eight characters. A string defined as

`"\\"`

will allow the first two characters of a string to be printed in a field, and using

`"!"`

allows only one character, the first. Conversely, using

`"&"`

allows all of the characters of a string to be printed.

Number fields:	Each digit of a number can be represented by a hash sign, #. Characters such as commas, decimal point and currency symbols can be placed in their correct position in relation to the digits, for example:

`"+###.##"`

defines a + sign, three digits ahead of the decimal point and two digits following the decimal point. A sign (+ or -) can be positioned before or following a number by placing the sign ahead or following the hash marks.

The currency sign can be placed ahead of the hashmarks, but only the dollar sign can be *floated* meaning that it will be placed just ahead of a number of any size. For example:

PRINT USING "$###,###.##"; 12.66

will produce:

$ 12.66

but when a double-dollar sign is used, one dollar sign will appear closed up against the first figure, so that:

PRINT USING "$$###,###.##"; 12.66

will produce:

$12.66

but this facility is not available for any other currency sign.

Asterisk signs can be used to replace leading spaces in a number, a device often used in cheque printing to avoid forgery. For example:

PRINT USING "##.##";6.772**

will produce:

***6.77

— note that only two decimal places are used because of the formatting string.

The currency sign and asterisk can be combined, so that:

PRINT USING "£###.##"; 5.32**

will produce:

£****5.32

A comma can be placed ahead of a decimal point in a formatting string to indicate that digits should be grouped in threes, so that:

PRINT USING "#####,.##"; 12176.55

will give:

12,176.55

Another special sign is the set of four carets (^^^^) which is used to indicate that a number should be formatted in scientific notation. For example:

PRINT USING "#.###^^^^" 1268

will produce:

1.268E3

Finally, using an underscore character ahead of any formatting character will cause that character to be printed as such, not causing a formatting effect.

PRINT USING _###.##"; 12.66

gives:

#12.66

Restrictions: The PRINT #2 USING type of output requires a file to be open. The floating dollar formatting string cannot easily be adapted to use any other currency symbol. If a number value is too large to fit into its specified field, a % sign will be printed ahead of the output to draw attention to the problem.

Examples:

(a) string fields

```
name$ = "Fielding, Henry"        'string to print
PRINT USING "\ \"; name$         'selects 5 characters
$ = "\ \"                        'longer field
PRINT USING f$; name$            'used here
PRINT USING "!"; name$           'single character
PRINT USING "&"; name$           'whole string
END
```

(b) number fields

```
CLS
FOR n% = 1 TO 5                  'five examples
  RESTORE forms                 'ready to read
  FOR x% = 1 TO n%              'start
    READ f$                     'read number
  NEXT                          'last in is used
  RESTORE nums                  'read numbers
  FOR j% = 1 TO 5              'one at a time
    READ d                      'number
    PRINT USING f$; d           'printed formatted
  NEXT                          'and so on
    SLEEP 1                     'wait
    PRINT
```

```
NEXT
END
forms:
DATA"##,###.##","##.#","#,###.#","#.#","#####"
nums:
DATA 1.57,11.236,10143.2,1071623,237.145
REM Prints a set of numbers, each set using a
REM different formatting string.
```

Associated with: LPRINT, OPEN, PRINT, WIDTH, WINDOW,

Points to note:

This is a neglected facility, mainly because only the dollar sign can be floated in contact with numbers. Nevertheless, PRINT USING can solve many print formatting problems simply and elegantly.

PSET

Type:	Statement
Typical syntax:	PSET (coordinates)
	PSET (coordinates),colour
Action:	Sets a pixel colour to the current foreground colour or to a specified new colour.
Options:	STEP placed ahead of co-ordinates makes all co-ordinates relative to the current cursor position. If no colour number is used the current foreground colour will be used.
Argument(s):	The co-ordinates, within brackets, are for a pixel on the graphics screen. A colour number can be used to set the pixel colour to this other colour.
Restrictions:	The colour default is the highest colour number that can be used for the screen mode. The co-ordinates must not fall outside the range permitted for the current SCREEN mode number.

Example:

```
SCREEN 12                    'VGA 640 x 480
CLS
FOR j& = 0 TO 307199         'cover whole screen
  y% = j& \ 640              'y from integer division
  x% = j& MOD 640            'x from remainder
  PSET (x%, y%)              'set this pixel
  IF y% > 239 THEN           'check position
     PRESET (x%, y% - 239)   'wipe out half screen up
  END IF
NEXT
```

Associated with: PRESET, SCREEN, VIEW, WINDOW

Points to note:

As the example illustrates, using PSET and PRESET to work on large areas can be very slow. This may be useable in some applications, but for drawings that need to be made rapidly, use the DRAW statement.

PUT (file statement)

Type: Statement

Typical syntax: PUT number

                      PUT number, record, variable

Action: Places data into an open random-access file either from a buffer or from a variable.

Options: Used with only a filenumber argument, PUT will select the next record position from the previous PUT or GET.

Argument(s):   The number is a file number, which can optionally use the hash marker, as in PUT #2, or PUT 2. The other arguments can specify the record number in a random-access file and the variable name which contains the data to be put into the file.

Restrictions: Older versions of BASIC did not use the variable option which makes possible the neater and simpler random-access filing system of QBASIC.

Example:

```
CLS
FILE% = 1                        'file handle number
LIMIT% = 100                     'maximum number of items
DIM A AS INTEGER
OPEN "integer.rnd" FOR RANDOM AS #FILE% LEN = 2 'open file
FOR n% = 1 TO LIMIT%
A% = 1000 - n%                   'recognisable number!
PUT FILE%, n%, A%                'put into next position in file
NEXT                             'and get the next
CLOSE
```

Associated with: FIELD, GET, LSET, OPEN, RANDOM, RSET

Points to note:

When the method involving the use of a variable is adopted, the use of the FIELD, LSET, RSET, MK$ and CV statements is made redundant. If the variable that is to be used contains sub-data (for example, two strings, one integer and one double-precision) it can be declared as a TYPE and a variable of that type used, avoiding the need for FIELD and all its associated statements.

PUT (graphics statement)

Type: Statement

Typical syntax: PUT (coordinates), array
PUT (coordinates), array (subscript)
PUT (coordinates),, action

Action: Reads the contents of an array on to the screen so as to reproduce an image pattern. The array will have been filled by using the graphics GET statement.

Options: STEP placed ahead of the co-ordinate values makes these relative to the current cursor position.

Argument(s): The co-ordinates are in normal x,y form, using values that depend on the screen type and window size, and they determine the position of the top lefthand corner of the corner of the picture. The array is one filled by using GET, and a specified starting subscript can be used. The co-ordinates must be enclosed in brakets.

The action option allows the array-image picture to be placed on the existing image, or modified according to the word used:

AND	Merges array-image with an existing image.
OR	Superimposes array-image on existing image.
PSET	Draws array-image, erasing existing image.
PRESET	Draws array-image in reverse colours, erasing existing image.
XOR	Draws array-image or erases a previously drawn image while preserving the background so as to animate the pictures.

Restrictions: The SCREEN mode used for PUT must be identical to the mode used for the corresponding GET.

Examples:

(a)
```
PUT (x%, y%), Pix%        'put image stored as array
                          'into position
```

(b)
```
DIM pix%(255)
SCREEN 1                  'low resolution
CIRCLE (15,15), 9, 1      'draw circle
GET (0,0) - (30,30), Pix% 'get into array
```

```
FOR j% = 1 TO 5            'start loop
  PUT (j% * 32, 80), Pix%  'put images back
NEXT                       'at different places
END
REM Error if PUT co-ordinates are outside screen
REM area for selected SCREEN number.
```

Associated with: SCREEN, DIM

Points to note:

This allows a graphics image to be rapidly placed in a specified position. See GET for details of how to calculate the dimensions of the array which is used to store the pattern. This array can be saved as a sequential or binary file so that screen patterns can be stored on disk and retrieved subsequently to be replaced with PUT. This technique is easier to use with high-resolution screens than BLOAD and BSAVE.

RANDOM

Type:	Statement
Typical syntax:	OPEN filename FOR RANDOM AS number
Action:	Causes a file to be opened as a random-access file. If no FOR clause is used, the default is a random-access file.
Options:	None.
Argument(s):	None.
Restrictions:	Can only be used as part of OPEN statement following FOR.

Example:

(a) A random access file reading routine for a file of integers using the older MKI$, CVI, LSET type of system.

```
OPEN "integer.rnd" FOR RANDOM AS #FILE% LEN = 2
REM Opens random access file of integers, previously
created
FIELD FILE%, 2 AS N$        '2 bytes per record
N% = 1                      'Section number
DO WHILE N% <> 0            'start loop
INPUT "Item number, please (0 to end) "; N%
GET FILE%, N%               'get requested item
X% = CVI(N$)               'convert stored string to integer
PRINT "Number is "; X%     'and print it
SLEEP 1                     'wait
CLS                         'clear
LOOP                        'next one
CLOSE                       'finished, close file
END
```

(b) A random-acess integer write and read pair of routines using the modern system of a declared type with extended PUT and GET statements

```
CLS
ON ERROR GOTO getout
REM Close file on error such as request for record zero
```

```
FILE% = 1: LIMIT% = 100      'set numbers to be used
DIM A AS INTEGER             'declare variable for file
OPEN "integer.rnd" FOR RANDOM AS #FILE% LEN = 2
REM Open random access file with 2-byte records
FOR n% = 1 TO LIMIT%         'start recording loop
A% = 1000 - n%:              'recognisable number for test
PUT FILE%, n%, A%            'place in file
NEXT                         'next one
CLOSE                        'end of recording
PRINT "Press any key to read" 'start reading
K$ = INPUT$(1)
OPEN "integer.rnd" FOR RANDOM AS #FILE% LEN = 2
REM Open file for reading - same syntax
n% = 1                       'file number dummy
DO WHILE n% <> 0             'start loop
INPUT "Item number, please (0 to end) "; n%
GET FILE%, n%, A%            'recover a record
PRINT "Number is "; A%       'print value
SLEEP 1                      'wait
CLS                          'clear
LOOP                         'next
getout:
CLOSE                        'close file
END
```

Associated with: GET, OPEN, PUT

Points to note:
The older type of random-access file, using the MK and CV form of
functions along with FIELD, LSET and RSET is now obsolete, and it is
available in QBASIC for compatibility with older BASIC versions only.
Modern programs should make use of the system outlined in Example (b),
in which the PUT and GET statements name a declared variable which is
used to carry data to or from the file. This variable can be a user-defined
type in which several number and string types are used, see TYPE.

RANDOMIZE

Type:	Statement
Typical syntax:	RANDOMIZE number
Action:	Seeds the random-number generator.
Options:	None.
Argument(s):	A seed number. If this is omitted, you will be prompted for one. Where reasonably random numbers are needed, using RANDOMIZE (TIMER) is a good method of ensuring a suitable seed number.
Restrictions:	None.

Example:

```
RANDOMIZE TIMER
PRINT "Press any key for random number (0 for end)
DO WHILE INPUT$(1) <> "0"
PRINT INT(RND * 100 + 1)
LOOP
```

Associated with: RND

Points to note:

A computer cannot generate a truly random number, because a formula is used to generate each number. If RANDOMIZE is not used, the RND function will always generate the same sequence of numbers. This in itself may be useful for testing, but not for any purpose that requires the number sequence to be different each time the computer is used.

By using RANDOMIZE along with a changing number such as TIMER, however, you can avoid RND generating sequences that repeat in any obvious way. The numbers are not random enough, however, for some statistical work (such as the Monte Carlo analysis method) that requires truly random numbers such as can be obtained from tables. For all but the most demanding uses, however, using RANDOMIZE TIMER gives results that are close enough to being random.

READ

Type:	Statement
Typical syntax:	READ variable
Action:	Reads items from a DATA list and assigns to a variable or to a set of variables.
Options:	None.
Argument(s):	A variable name or list of variable names separated by using a comma.
Restrictions:	A READ produces an Out of Data error (error 4) if all the list has already been read. Reading must be done to the correct type of variable, see Notes.

Examples:

(a)
```
FOR N% = 1 TO 10          'read ten items in loop
   READ A$                'each as a string
   PRINT A$               'and print
NEXT
DATA Jim,22.5,"Hodge, T.X.", 33.8, Paul, 55.6, Sally,
22.4, Sue, 23.6
REM Note use of quotes for item containing a comma.
```

(b)
```
CLS
READ A$,B!, C%, D#        'four variable types
PRINT A$; " ";B!          'print the
PRINT C%; " ";D#          'results here
DATA Specification numbers, 26.78, 14, 127593.739
REM Numbers must be read into the correct variable types
```

(c) Using RESTORE.
```
CLS
PRINT "Which list do you want (1 to 3)?"
PRINT
DO
   INPUT a%                        'pick list number
LOOP UNTIL a% > 0 AND a% < 4
IF a% = 1 THEN RESTORE british     'use this data list
IF a% = 2 THEN RESTORE german      'or this one
```

```
IF a% = 3 THEN RESTORE italian        'or this one
FOR n% = 1 TO 4: READ a$(n%): NEXT    'read them
PRINT "Now pick a number, 1 to 4"     'pick item from list
  INPUT x%                            'make choice
LOOP UNTIL x% > 0 AND x% < 5          'get correct range
PRINT a$(x%)                          'print item
british:                              'lists follow
DATA Rover, Aston-Martin, Jaguar, Vauxhall
german:
DATA BMW, Mercedes, Porsche, Opel
italian:
DATA Alfa Romeo, Fiat, Lancia, Ferrari
```

Assiciated with: DATA, RESTORE

Points to note:

When more than one line of DATA exists and the lines are named by labels, the RESTORE statement can be used to force a selected data line to be used by READ. This is illustrated in Example (c).

A number variable can read only a number, and if any attempt is made to read a string the program will refuse to run, with a Syntax Error message displayed.

A string variable can be used to read any type of data.

If data includes a comma, the whole of the data must be enclosed in quotes so that the comma is not taken as the separator between data items.

The RESTORE statement can be used as a method of selecting alternative data sets, as illustrated, or in a form of menu system.

REDIM

Type:	Statement
Typical syntax:	REDIM array(subscript)
	REDIM array(subscript) AS type
Action:	Redefines a dynamic array, making the redefined array also dynamic (see Appendix B).
Options:	SHARED placed before the variable or array name ensures that the values will be global, shared with all subroutines and functions.
Argument(s):	A scalar or array variable name can be used. To redimension an array, you can use either the upper limit of subscript for each dimension, or the syntax lower TO upper for each to specify both lower and upper limits.
	The variable or array can also be declared as being of a type if the name does not include a marker such as !, #, %, $ etc. The types are INTEGER, LONG, SINGLE, DOUBLE, STRING, or a user-defined type (record).
Restrictions:	Only an array that has originally been declared as dynamic can be redimensioned using REDIM. A static array is fixed for the duration of the program and cannot be redimensioned

Example:

```
CLS
a% = 5                   'assign variable
DIM g%(a%)               'using a% makes array dynamic
FOR n% = 1 TO a%         'fill it
  READ g%(a%)            'from data line
  PRINT g%(a%); " ";     'and print
NEXT
SLEEP 1                  'wait
PRINT                    'new line
a% = 8                   'new dimension
REDIM g%(a%)             'redimension array
FOR n% = 1 TO a%         'and fill it
  READ g%(a%)            'with new numbers
```

```
      PRINT g%(a%); " ";     'and print them
   NEXT
   END
   DATA 1,2,3,4,5,6,7,8,9,10,11,12,13
```

Assiciated with: COMMON, ERASE, OPTION BASE, SHARED, STATIC, $STATIC, $DYNAMIC,

Points to note:

REDIM is not a statement that should be needed in more than a handful of programs, and you should think carefully about its use. In particular, when an array is redimensioned any values that were stored in the array are cleared. This prevents REDIM from being used in the most obvious application, of defining an array as dynamic in order to receive items from a file, making the size of the array intentionally very large and redimensioning it when the a number of items is known.

You can, however, read in items to a large array, find the number of items, and then store them in another array which can be dimensioned to the correct size, then clear the original array. This takes advantage of dynamic arrays to create and release arrays in the course of the program, unlike static arrays. For example:

```
CLS
REM $DYNAMIC              'all arrays dynamic
DIM g% (1000)            'big array
OPEN "numtest" FOR INPUT AS #2   'open file of integers
n% = 1                   'counter
DO                       'reading loop
  INPUT #2, g%(n%)       'get number and assign
  n% = n% + 1            'increment counter
LOOP UNTIL EOF(2)        'until end of file
n% = n% - 1              'correct number
DIM h%(n%)               'new array of this size
FOR j% = 1 TO n%         'loop to
  h%(j%) = g%(j%)        'transfer numbers
NEXT                     'to new array
ERASE g%                 'get rid of old one
FOR k% = 1 TO n%         'now print
PRINT h%(k%); " ";       'the lot
NEXT
END
```

REM

Type:	Statement
Typical syntax:	REM This is the main input step
	' An alternative REM
Action:	Allows comments to be made, or temporarily prevents a line from being executed. Used also for metacommands such as $DYNAMIC, $STATIC.
Options:	None.
Argument(s):	None.
Restrictions:	Everything following a REM or ' is normally ignored up to a carriage-return. This does not apply to metacommands that start with the dollar sign.

Examples:

(a)   `REM This is a comment in a line of its own`

(b)   `PRINT A 'prints data comment follows statement`
       `PRINT A : REM Colon needed if REM form used`

(c)   `REM FOR n% = 1 TO 1000`
         `REM PRINT K(n%)`
       `REM NEXT`
       `REM we don't want these lines to run while`
       `REM we are testing the program. Take the REMS`
       `REM out later when the program is working`

(d)   `REM $DYNAMIC`
       `REM all arrays will be dynamic`

Assiciated with: $STATIC, $DYNAMIC

Points to note:

A REM following a statement must be separated either by using a colon (as for a multistatement line) or by using the ' form of REM.

RESET

Type:	Statement
Typical syntax:	RESET
Action:	Closes all open files or devices.
Options:	None.
Argument(s):	None.
Restrictions:	None.

Example:

```
OPEN "myfile" FOR INPUT AS #1      'open sequential 1
OPEN "newfile" FOR OUTPUT AS #2    'open sequential 2
OPEN "oldfile" FOR BINARY AS #3    'open binary 3
OPEN "PRN:" FOR OUTPUT AS #4       'printer is #4
...................                'other statements
RESET                              'close all files
```

Assiciated with: CLOSE, END, OPEN, STOP

Points to note:

RESET performs the same action as CLOSE but without requiring any arguments. Using RESET ensures that all buffers are written (flushed) before closing. This is a useful way of ensuring that all file data is written to the disk and that the MS-DOS directory will be updated. Note that END, CLOSE, RUN and STOP also close all open files and devices.

RESUME

Type: Statement

Typical syntax: RESUME 0
                     RESUME NEXT
                     RESUME position

Action: Used in error trapping routines.

RESUME and RESUME 0 forces the program to resume at the statement that caused the error.

RESUME NEXT forces the program to resume on the statement following the statement which caused the error.

RESUME *position* is used with a label to cause the program to be resumed at the statement following the label name.

Options: Can be used with or without an argument as listed above.

Argument(s):   See Action list above.

Restrictions: RESUME has to be used as part of an ON ERROR GOTO routine. If RESUME is found in any other part of a program, the *Resume Without Error* message (error 20) appears and the program stops.

Examples:

(a)
```
ON ERROR GOTO sortit           'define error-handler
PRINT "Type a word, please"    'try a null-string
INPUT a$
L% = LEN(a$)                   'word length
PRINT 1/L%                     'OK if not null string
PRINT "END"
END
sortit:                        'error handler
PRINT "Word has no letters!"   '1/L% impossible
RESUME NEXT                    'prints END
```

(b)
```
ON ERROR GOTO sortit           'define error-handler
starter:                       'label for resume
PRINT "Type a word, please"    'try a null-string
```

```
INPUT a$
L% = LEN(a$)                        'word length
PRINT 1/L%                          'OK if not null string
PRINT "END"
END
sortit:                             'error handler
PRINT "Word has no letters!"        'message
RESUME starter                      'try again
```

Assiciated with: ERDEV, ERDEV$, ERR, ON ERROR GOTO

Points to note:

See Error number list, Appendix E, for ERR numbers that can be tested and used to determine the action required before a RESUME is used. If no RESUME is used, the error handling routine will require an END if it is not placed at the end of the program – since ON ERROR uses a GOTO, there is no automatic return to the program other than by using RESUME. You should not be tempted to end an error routine with another GOTO.

RESTORE

Type: Statement

Typical syntax: RESTORE
RESTORE lineref

Action: Restores a data read list to the start, or starts reading data at a specified line label or number.

Options: None.

Argument(s): A line number or label name can be used to point to a specific data line. If no reference is used, the first DATA line in the program will be used again after a RESTORE has been encountered.

Restrictions: None.

Examples:

(a)
```
:errorsub
IF ERR = 4          'out of data
RESTORE             're-start data list
RESUME              'back to program
```

(b)
```
RESTORE             'in case a READ has been used earlier
FOR j% = 1 TO 20    'read list
READ A$(j%)         'of string items
NEXT
```

(c)
```
CLS
PRINT "Which list do you want (1 to 3)?"
PRINT
DO
   INPUT a%                           'pick list number
LOOP UNTIL a% > 0 AND a% < 4
IF a% = 1 THEN RESTORE british        'use this data list
IF a% = 2 THEN RESTORE german         'or this one
IF a% = 3 THEN RESTORE italian        'or this one
FOR n% = 1 TO 4: READ a$(n%): NEXT    'read them
PRINT "Now pick a number, 1 to 4"     'pick item from list
DO
   INPUT x%                           'make choice
```

```
LOOP UNTIL x% > 0 AND x% < 5        'get correct range
PRINT a$(x%)                        'print item
british:                            'lists follow
DATA Rover, Aston-Martin, Jaguar, Vauxhal
german:
DATA BMW, Mercedes, Porsche, Opel
italian:
DATA Alfa Romeo, Fiat, Lancia, Ferrari
```

Associated with: DATA, READ

Points to note:

RESTORE used in the way illustrated in example (c) provides a form of menu routine, or a way of allowing groups to be selected, such as words to be used in messages (select language), lists of spare parts (select model) and so on.

RETURN

Type:	Statement
Typical syntax:	RETURN
	RETURN lineref
Action:	Terminates a GOSUB subroutine action and returns either to the next instruction or to a nominated line.
Options:	None.
Argument(s):	Line number or label can be used; the default is the next statement that can be executed.
Restrictions:	See GOSUB.

Example:

```
CLS
t$ = "Practical PC"              'string to centre
GOSUB centre                     'call routine
t$ = STRING$(LEN(t$), "-")       'another string
GOSUB centre                     'call again
END                              'important!
centre:                          'subroutine
nr% = LEN(t$)                    'calculate position
PRINT TAB((80 - nr%) / 2); t$    'print
RETURN                           'back to program
```

Associated with: GOSUB

Points to note:

Modern programs should use SUB and CALL in preference to GOSUB…RETURN.

The use of RETURN with a nominated line label or number is not common in BASIC, and should be used with caution, since it is subject to the same abuses as the use of GOTO. If you use QBASIC programs that have RETURN statements with nominated lines you will find these difficult to convert to other versions of BASIC.

RIGHT$

Type:	Function
Typical syntax:	PRINT RIGHT$(string, number)
Action:	Returns a copy of part of the argument string, counting characters from the righthand side up to the specified argument number.
Options:	None.
Argument(s):	String to be slice-copied, and the position number from righthand side of string to specify slicing position, all within brackets and separated by a comma.
Restrictions:	The position number should not be larger than the size of string. The position number cannot exceed 32767.

Examples:

(a)
```
Allname$ = "Clarence C. Postlethwaite"
PRINT RIGHT$(Allname$, 10)
REM Prints tlethwaite
REM this could be enough to identify the string
REM using INSTR$
```

(b)
```
INPUT "Type code number and press ENTER key", code$
X$ = RIGHT$(code$,5)
X = VAL(X$)
IF X <> 27895 THEN
    PRINT "No admission"
    END
END IF
```

Associated with: LEFT$, MID$

Points to note:

The string which is being sliced is not affected or altered in any way unless its variable name is reassigned.

If the position number is larger than the number of characters in the string, the whole string is copied. If the position number is zero the copy is a null string (no characters).

RMDIR

Type:	Statement
Typical syntax:	RMDIR dirname$
Action:	Removes a sub-directory.
Options:	None.
Argument(s):	Directory name must be in string format, either as a literal (name in quotes) or a string variable.
Restrictions:	The directory must exist. A directory cannot be removed if it contains any files or has any subdirectories. The root directory cannot be removed.

Examples:

```
RMDIR "C:\QBASIC\OLDEXMP"
```

Associated with: CHDIR, FILES, KILL, MKDIR, NAME

Points to note:

It should seldom be necessary to remove a directory from within a BASIC program except when the BASIC program has created a temporary directory for use by the program.

RND

Type:	Function returning double-precision fraction
Typical syntax:	variable = RND(number)
Action:	Returns a fraction between 0 and 1.
Options:	None.
Argument(s):	A number used as an argument, placed inside brackets, can be negative, zero, or positive.
	With a negative argument, RND always returns the same number, unaffected by the actual value of argument or the use of RANDOMIZE.
	With a zero argument, RND also keeps returning the last number that was generated, but this will be a different number each time the program is run provided RANDOMIZE is used.
	With a positive argument, RND generates a new random number each time it is used.
Restrictions:	The number that is returned is not truly random, see the entry for RANDOMIZE.

Example:

```
RANDOMIZE TIMER              'ensure new sequence
PRINT "Press any key for random number (0 for end)"
DO WHILE INPUT$(1) <> "0"
PRINT INT(RND * 100 + 1)    'use random fraction to create
LOOP                        'number between 1 and 100
```

Associated with: RANDOMIZE

Points to note:

Since the number that RND produces is always a double-precision fraction (always less than 1), the general method of producing a set of random numbers between 1 and N% is to use:

$$INT(RND * N\%) + 1$$

and this can be made into a defined function if integer random numbers in a specified range are needed at various parts of a program.

RSET

Type:	Function
Typical syntax:	RSET field$ = variable$
Action:	Sets a string to the righthand side of a field for use in a random-access file.
Options:	None.
Argument(s):	A string declared in a FIELD statement and a variable to assign, separated by a comma.
Restrictions:	The field$ name must have been declared in the FIELD statement.

Examples:

```
OPEN "randfil" AS #1 LEN = 14        'prepare file
FIELD #1, 2 as Nr%, 4 as sing!, 8 AS doub#   'record defined
RSET Nr% = MKI$(5)                   'integer field
RSET sing! = MKS$(2.6)               'single field
RSET doub# = MKD$(3.66)              'double field
PUT #1,1                             'save as record 1
CLOSE                                'close
```

Associated with: FIELD, LSET

Points to note:

Modern programs should use a defined record type rather than the old FILE, LSET, RSET form of commands. See under RANDOM for an example of an integer file using the modern system.

RTRIM$

Type:	Function returning string
Typical syntax:	variable = RTRIM$(string)
Action:	Removes any spaces from the righthand side of a string.
Options:	None.
Argument(s):	The string from which spaces are to be removed, enclosed in brackets.
Restrictions:	None.

Example:

```
CLS
nam$ = "    Sinclair    "    'string with spaces
end$ = " Books"               'single space
PRINT nam$ + end$             'see what it looks like
PRINT LTRIM$(nam$) + end$     'trim left
PRINT RTRIM$(nam$) + end$     'trim right
a$ = LTRIM$(nam$)             'assign left-trimmed
a$ = RTRIM$(a$)               'and now right trimmed
PRINT a$ + end$              'and print result
```

Associated with: LTRIM$

Points to note:
This can be a very useful way of removing padding space from strings that are returned from a random-access file. It can also be useful when strings are entered from the keyboard with unwanted spaces, but it cannot remove unwanted spaced from between words. For such an action, a loop is required which uses MID$ to look for double spaces and will reduce a double space to a single space.

RUN

Type:	Statement
Typical syntax:	RUN "filename"
	RUN line
Action:	Runs another program, or runs from a specified line in the current program. The memory is cleared before the new RUN starts.
Options:	RUN *line* can be used only if line numbering is used, otherwise the RUN starts at the first line (other than a REM).
Argument(s):	Line number if running is to start in the current program.
Restrictions:	The full filename must be supplied, particularly for an EXE or BAT form of file. The RUN *line* option can use only a line number, not a label name.

Examples:

(a)   `RUN "C:\QBASIC\MYPROG.BAS"` `'runs named program`

(b)   `RUN 100`   `'starts current program at 100`

(c)   `RUN "GETEM.BAT"`   `'runs batch file`

Associated with: CHAIN

Points to note:

Seldom needed. The RUN line-number form is obsolete.

For many applications, if one BASIC program is to run another you will usually want some variables to retain their values to be used in the second program, so that the CHAIN statement along with COMMON is more desirable.

SCREEN function

Type:	Function returning number
Typical syntax:	SCREEN (position)
	SCREEN (position, option)
Action:	Returns a number representing the ASCII value or the colour attribute of a character at a specified position on the text screen.
Options:	An option number can be used following the column number, using 0 to return the ASCII code, 1 to return the colour attribute.
Argument(s):	The position is determined by the row and column number in that order, separated by a comma. If no option number is used, the default is to return the ASCII code. The arguments must be enclosed in the brackets.
Restrictions:	Only option numbers 0 and 1 are acceptable.

Example:

```
LOCATE 5, 8              'position cursor
PRINT "HERE"            'place characters
PRINT SCREEN (5, 8)     'ASCII code for C is 67
PRINT SCREEN (5, 8, 1)  'colour code
```

Associated with: POINT, SCREEN Statement

Points to note:

This is used on the text screen to provide the same action as POINT performs in the graphics screen. It can be used to find a given letter or colour attribute by using a loop that covers all of the possible LOCATE numbers, but this is a slow action.

SCREEN statement

Type: Statement

Typical syntax: SCREEN modenumber
       SCREEN modenumber, colour
       SCREEN modenumber, colour, page1
       SCREEN modenumber, colour, page1, page2

Action: Sets the screen mode (resolution) for text and graphics. See Appendix E for details of all screen modes available in QBASIC.

Options: The colour number (0 or 1 only) is used only for CGA screens to enable or disable colour:

Mode	colour number	Action
0	0	Disables colour
0	Not zero	Enables colour
1	0	Enables colour
1	Not zero	Disables colour

Argument(s): The mode number determines the mode, normally 12, for the high-resolution VGA screen and mode 0 for the normal text screen.

       The page1 number is the number of the screen page that is currently being used to write text or graphics output.

       The page2 number is the number of the screen page that is currently being displayed.

Restrictions: The number of possible screen pages depends on screen mode and memory. See Appendix F for details of screen modes and video pages. If an intermediate option is not used, the commas must not be omitted.

Example:

```
SCREEN 1,0                '320 x 200 low-resolution
CIRCLE (100,100,),50,2    'draw circle, colour 2
INPUT$(1)                 'wait for key
SCREEN 0,0,0,0,           'text screen, page 0
INPUT$(1)                 'wait for key
SCREEN ,,2                'text screen, page 2
```

```
INPUT$(1)                'wait for key
SCREEN 12                '640 x 480 high-resolution
CIRCLE (320,200),100.1   'draw circle
END
```

Associated with: CIRCLE, COLOR, DRAW, LINE, PAINT, SCREEN
Function, VIEW, WINDOW

Points to note:

The colour number in the SCREEN statement is not intended to control the colours of text or graphics, only to enable or disable colour options in other statements such as LINE or CIRCLE. The colours that you can specify in these statements depend on the type of graphics card you are using. The standard form of VGA card is the highest resolution that can be supported at present.

The screen pages allow text or graphics to be prepared on a page that is not currently being displayed. Switching pages with a SCREEN statement then allows a switch of displayed page, so replacing one complete screen view by another. Switching between pages can be used as a (rather limited) method of animation, but is available only on the lower-resolution screen modes.

SEEK function

Type:	Function returning integer number
Typical syntax:	SEEK(filenumber)
Action:	Returns the position of a record or byte in the currently used open file. The position number for a random access file is the record number; for all other file types it is the byte position number. Position numbers start from 1, not from 0.
Options:	None.
Argument(s):	The number of an open file, without the hash sign. and enclosed in brackets.
Restrictions:	The file must be opened.

Example:

```
CLS
OPEN "numtest" FOR INPUT AS #1        'a file of integers
FOR n% = 1 TO 4                       'first four
PRINT SEEK(1); " ";                   'find position
INPUT #1, a%                          'read
PRINT a%; " ";                        'print number
NEXT
CLOSE
END
REM This prints, for a file of consecutive number 1,2,3, etc
REM the output 1 1 6 2 11 3 16 4
REM showing 4 bytes used for each number in this file
```

Associated with: SEEK Statement

Points to note:
The sequential file example above shows that the file allowed space for a long integer, with four bytes allocated for each number. This illustrates the use of SEEK as a valuable method for checking how file space is allocated.

SEEK statement

Type:	Statement
Typical syntax:	SEEK filenumber, position
Action:	Sets the next file position for a read or write.
	Random access file – sets to the record number used as a file position argument
	All others – sets to the byte number (starting at 1) specified by the position number.
Options:	None.
Argument(s):	The filenumber is the number established by the OPEN statement, with or without the hash sign. The position number for a random access file is the record number; for all other file types it is the byte position number. Position numbers start from 1, not from 0.
Restrictions:	The file must already be open. The position number must correspond to a place in the file – if you have opened a random-access file for 100 records and you write a record at position 110 you are likely to corrupt the disk, possibly writing over another file on the disk.

Example:

```
CLS
OPEN "numtest" FOR INPUT AS #1    'open file of integers
SEEK 1, 6                         'position 6th byte
INPUT #1, x%                      'get the number
PRINT x%                          'and print it
END
```

Associated with: GET, OPEN, PUT

Points to note:

The use of SEEK is not so important in QBASIC as in older forms of BASIC, with which the SEEK statement maintains compatibility. The GET and PUT statements of QBASIC allow the position in the file to be specified, making the use of SEEK redundant for this purpose.

SELECT

Type: Statement

Typical syntax: SELECT CASE expression
                                CASE item1
                                Statement 1
                                Case item2
                                Statement 2
                                CASE ELSE
                                Statement alternative
               END SELECT

Action: Carries out a menu action by listing criteria for selection and their appropriate actions.

Options: CASE *item* is used to select a course of action for one argument or a range specified by using a dash. For example, CASE 5 and CASE 1 4 are valid uses of this option.

CASE IS must be used if what follows is a relationship using any of the operators = , <, or >. For example, CASE IS A% => 10 or CASE IS N% <>5 are valid uses of this for.

CASE ELSE is used to provide an action for all numbers or strings that are not provided for in other parts of the CASE list.

Argument(s): The expression argument can be a number or a string, usually entered from the keyboard or a file.

Restrictions: If there are any items not covered by CASE they will be dealt with by CASE ELSE.

Examples:

(a)
```
CLS
PRINT "Please pick by number, range 1 to 3, 0 to end"
DO
    INPUT N%                    'get menu item number
    SELECT CASE N%              'select by this
       CASE IS < 1              'if less than 1
          EXIT DO               'get out
       CASE 1                   'if 1
```

```
      PRINT "First choice"            'do this
   CASE 2                             'if 2
      PRINT "Second choice"           'do this
   CASE 3                             'if 3
      PRINT "Third choice"            'do this
   CASE IS > 3                        'higher numbers
      PRINT "Out of range - please try again."
   END SELECT                         'mark end
LOOP                                  'infinite loop
REM Note that entering 0 or any number less than
REM 1 is the only way out of the loop.
```

(b)
```
DECLARE SUB savit ()                'declare subs
DECLARE SUB usit ()                 'which are, in fact
DECLARE SUB setitup ()              'dummy routines
CLS
PRINT "please select by name -"     'not number this time
PRINT "setup, use, record, leave"   'list of names
INPUT reply$                         'string entry
SELECT CASE reply$                   'used in SELECT CASE
  CASE "setup"                       'first item
    CALL setitup                     'and its SUB
  CASE "use"                         'second item
    CALL usit                        'and its SUB
  CASE "record"                      'third item
    CALL savit                       'and its SUB
  CASE "leave"                       'get out
    PRINT "leaving now"              'with message
  CASE ELSE                          'any other item
    PRINT "No choice made"           'causes this
END SELECT                           'and ends it

SUB savit                            'list of the
PRINT "Saving file"                  'dummy SUBS
END SUB                              'which must exist
SUB setitup                          'to make the
PRINT "Set up being done"            'example work
```

```
END SUB
SUB usit
PRINT "Using routine"
END SUB
```

Associated with: CASE, ON…GOSUB, ON…GOTO

Points to note:

You can use lines such as:

CASE 1,4,8 or CASE able, baker, charlie

in which more than one input item will trigger an action. You can also use a range such as

CASE 1 TO 5   CASE CHARLIE TO JULIET

The CASE SELECT statement should be used in place of ON GOTO or ON GOSUB for menu actions in modern programs, and can also replace elaborate IF…THEN…ELSE clauses. The ON…GOSUB and ON…GOTO statements should be regarded as obsolescent, provided for compatibility only.

SGN

Type:	Function returning signed integer number 4
Typical syntax:	variable1 = SGN(variable2)
Action:	Returns a number that depends on the sign of the argument. The range is -1, 0 or +1 as follows:

Argument	SNG returns
negative	-1
zero	0
positive	+1

Options:	None.
Argument(s):	The argument can be any number, number variable or an expression that yields a number, enclosed in brackets.
Restrictions:	None.

Example:

```
INPUT "number, please", A$
X = VAL(A$)
IF SGN(X) = -1 THEN PRINT "Number is negative
IF SGN(X) = 0 THEN PRINT "You entered zero"
ELSE PRINT "Number is positive"
```

Associated with: ABS

Points to note:

An odd and interesting use of SGN is to provide a three-way selection based on the entry of zero, a positive number or a negative number, by using SGN in a SELECT CASE line. For example:

```
INPUT "Integer number, please (positive, zero or negative)";X%
SELECT CASE SGN(X%)              'select clause
   CASE 1                       'answers must be 1, -1 or 0
     PRINT "This is positive"   'dummy clause here
   CASE 1                       'negative
     PRINT "This is negative"
   CASE 0                       'zero not strictly needed
     PRINT "This is zero"
END SELECT
REM Note that this always creates a 3-way select, because
REM the return from SGN can be one of only three possibilities
```

SHARED

Type:　　　　　　Statement

Typical syntax:　　SHARED variable, variable

　　　　　　　　　　SHARED variable AS type, variable AS type

Action:　　　　　Declares variables, optionally with type, which all procedures will have access to (global variables).

Options:　　　　A variable type can be declared, avoiding the use of marker characters such as !, #, %, $ and so on.

Argument(s):　　The variable name, which can be any valid name, see Appendix G.

Restrictions:　　The name used for a variable whose type is declared in this way *cannot* use a suffix. For example, it is illegal to use:

　　　　　　　　　　SHARED Able$ AS INTEGER, Baker% AS LONG

Examples:

(a)
```
DECLARE SUB demo ()
CLS
DIM SHARED n%              'this makes n% global
n% = 10
CALL demo
PRINT "a% outside is"; a% 'zero, this is local to procedure
PRINT "b% outside is"; b% 'likewise
END

SUB demo
a% = 2 * n%               'n% has a value - it is global
b% = 3 * n%               'likewise
PRINT "a% inside is"; a%  'a% is local
PRINT "b% inside is"; b%  'so is b%
END SUB
```

(b)
```
DIM SHARED n AS INTEGER    'makes this global
n = 5                     'assign
CALL useen               'call SUB

SUB useen
PRINT "n is "; n          'check value available
```

```
PRINT "in SUB useen"
j% = 2 * n                    'new variable
CALL inner                    'new SUB
END SUB

SUB inner
SHARED j%                     'so j% can be used
PRINT "j% is ";j%             'in this routine
PRINT "inside inner SUB"
END SUB
REM j% has no value in the main program unless it is
REM declared as SHARED in SUB useen.
```

Associated with: AS, COMMON, STATIC

Points to note:

SHARED has to be used with care to ensure that the sharing is as you expect.

1. If you use DIM SHARED in a main program, this makes the variable global, so that it can be used by all SUBs.

2. If you attempt to use SHARED without DIM in a main program, this will be rejected by the Editor.

3. If you use SHARED in a SUB, this makes a variable useable by the routine that called the SUB, not by a routine that the SUB calls.

SHELL

Type:	Statement
Typical syntax:	SHELL commandstring
Action:	Breaks out of the BASIC program to run a DOS command or a batch file. When the command or batch file is completed, the program resumes.
Options:	None.
Argument(s):	The commandstring is a DOS command in quotes, or a batch file name, also in quotes. A suitably-assigned string variable can be used.
Restrictions:	If no command is given, the DOS prompt appears and awaits a direct command. In this case, EXIT has to be typed and the ENTER key pressed to return to the BASIC program.

Example:

```
PRINT "Now copy this file to a floppy"
PRINT "You will return to BASIC afterwards"
SHELL "COPY SAMPLE.BAT A:"
PRINT "Action complete, back to BASIC"
END
```

Associated with: CHDIR, ENVIRON, ENVIRON$, FILES, MKDIR, NAME, RMDIR

Points to note:

You can *shell out* to any EXE, COM or BAT type of program, referred to as a *child program* of the BASIC program. The return to BASIC is always automatic provided that you have specified a program in the SHELL statement, see Restrictions.

SIN

Type: Function returning double-precision number.

Typical syntax: variable = SIN(angle)

Action: Returns the value of the sine of the angle used as an argument, and enclosed in brackets. See Appendix A for angles and trigonometrical functions.

Options: None.

Argument(s): An angle in units of radians as a number, number-variable or expression. The argument must be enclosed in brackets.

Restrictions: Values for angles very close to zero or to PI/2 (90°) are unreliable. Use A * PI / 180 for angle A in degrees, with PI defined as 3.1416.

Example:

```
SIDE = HYPOT * SIN(angle)    'find length of this side
CONST PI = 3.1416            'for conversion
FOR ang% = 5 TO 85 STEP 5    'prints a table of cosines
   PRINT "Angle"; ang%; "      Sine ";SIN(ang% * PI / 180)
NEXT
```

Associated with: ATN, COS, TAN

Points to note:

Very small angles give unreliable results, as do angles which are close to 90° or multiples of 90° (any multiple of PI/2 radians). The conversions between radians and degrees should be carried out using defined functions. The value of PI should be taken as 3.1416 unless high precision is needed.

SLEEP

Type:	Statement
Typical syntax:	SLEEP (number)
Action:	Suspends any program action for a stipulated number of seconds, or until a key is pressed.
Options:	The argument can be omitted, or zero used. This will cause the SLEEP action to continue until a key is pressed.
Argument(s):	The argument can be an integer or long integer, enclosed by brackets, and is the number of seconds to suspend program action.
Restrictions:	The number used as an argument cannot operate as a time number if it is zero or fractional, and if such a number is used the program will sleep indefinitely until a key is pressed.

Examples:

(a)
```
PRINT "Please wait"
SLEEP 2
PRINT "Now ready for action"
```

(b)
```
PRINT "Press any key"
SLEEP 0
```

Associated with: None.

Points to note:

The use of SLEEP is preferable to using a FOR...NEXT loop as a long time delay, because SLEEP will provide a time delay that is taken from the computer's clock system. This ensures that computers which run at very different speeds will provide the same delay for a given SLEEP statement. This is not the case when a FOR...NEXT loop is used, because the speed of the loop will be faster for a computer running at a higher clock rate.

Because SLEEP cannot use a number less than zero, delays of less than one second will still need to be supplied by using FOR...NEXT loops.

SOUND

Type:	Statement
Typical syntax:	SOUND frequency, time
Action:	Creates a sound whose frequency (related to pitch) and duration is controlled by numbers. Intended for sound effects rather than for music.
Options:	None.
Argument(s):	The frequency number (range 32 to 32767) is the frequency of the sound in Hertz. The time number can use the range 0 to 65535 and is in units of ticks with 18.2 *ticks* per second, so that a value of 18 provides a note of slightly less than one second duration.
Restrictions:	Numbers lower than 100 provide frequencies that are audible only through large loudspeakers, numbers greater than about 15,000 provide frequencies that are audible only to dogs. The duration numbers can range from about 0.0015 to 65535.

Examples:

```
(a)   FOR N% = 37 TO 10000   'large range of SOUND numbers
          SOUND N%, 1         'use each in turn
      NEXT                    'for a sliding note

(b)   FOR N% = 1 TO 36        'loop determines time
          SOUND 264, 1        'note 1
          SOUND 330, 1        'note 2
      NEXT                    'loop back
      REM creates a warbling note
```

Associated with: PLAY

Points to note:

SOUND is a useful way of producing sounds that are not strictly musical and which cannot be expressed in terms of musical notes (like much of modern music?). It can also be useful as a way of producing a sound of exact pitch. For example, SOUND 440,90 gives you five seconds of standard orchestral A and allows you to dispense with tuning forks if you happen to use them.

Using SOUND does not hold up the action of the machine because the SOUND action is independent of other BASIC actions. One SOUND statement must be completed, however, before another one can be started.

SPACE$

Type:	Function returning string
Typical syntax:	stringvariable = SPACE$(number)
Action:	Returns a string consisting of a specified number of spaces.
Options:	None.
Argument(s):	The number of spaces required, in the range 1 to 65535, enclosed in brackets.
Restrictions:	Avoid using very large numbers because the string space assigned in the memory may not be enough.

Example:

```
PRINT "LEFT"; SPACE$(15); "ONE"; SPACE$(15);
PRINT "TWO"; SPACE$(15);"RIGHT"
```

Associated with: SPC$, STRING$

Points to note:

This is a useful way of creating spaces, particularly for programs that are to be printed. It is always much easier to read a SPACE$ line than one which contains a space, because the number used with SPACE$ is unequivocal, counting the number of spaces in a line is not.

SPC

Type:	Function returning string
Typical syntax:	SPC(number)
Action:	Prints a specified number of spaces between text or number items.
Options:	None.
Argument(s):	The number of spaces between printed items, enclosed in brackets.
Restrictions:	Used only along with PRINT or LPRINT to provide spaces.

Example:

```
CLS
PRINT TAB(2); "BIG"; TAB(20); "BASIC"  'B at position 20
PRINT TAB(2); "BIG"; SPC(20); "BASIC"  'B 20 spaces beyond G
```

Associated with: LPRINT, LPRINT USING, PRINT, PRINT USING, SPACE$, TAB

Points to note:

Note that SPC can be used to place a specified number of spaces between items, whereas TAB is used to make each item start at a pre-selected point.

SQR

Type: Function returning double-precision number

Typical syntax: variable = SQR(number)

Action: Returns the square root of the number used as the argument. The returned number will be double-precision unless assigned to a variable of lower precision.

Options: None.

Argument(s):   The number whose square root is to be found, enclosed in brackets.

Restrictions: Error number 5, *Illegal Function Call*, is generated if the number argument is negative.

Examples:

```
PRINT "Square root of 5 is ";SQR(5)
A# = SQR(5): PRINT A#          'full precision
A! = A#                        'convert to single
PRINT A!                       'and print
X% = SQR(26): PRINT X%         'integer variable
REM note that using an integer variable will not
REM generally give the correct value because
REM of rounding to an integer
```

Associated with: EXP, LOG

Points to note:

The use of SQR is faster than the alternative of using a power of 0.5 in a line such as:

```
PRINT 5 ^ .5
```

but this type of action will be needed for any other roots such as cube roots, which require a line such as:

```
PRINT A
```

STATIC

Type:	Statement
Typical syntax:	STATIC variable, variable,…
	STATIC variable AS type, variable AS type,…
Action:	Declares a variable name or list of variable names, optionally with types, which will be local in a procedure but whose values are preserved between calls to the procedure.
Options:	The variable type can be declared, avoiding the use of marker characters such as !, #, %, $ and so on. The type can be INTEGER, LONG, SINGLE, DOUBLE, STRING, or a user-defined type.
Argument(s):	Variable names and, optionally, types as a list with items separated by commas.
Restrictions:	A name used for a variable whose type is declared in this way cannot use a suffix. For example, it is illegal to use:

```
STATIC Able$ AS INTEGER, Baker% AS LONG
```

Example:

```
DIM SHARED N%                    'N% is global
N% = 5                           'value is 5
CALL daftsub                     'prints 5 x 1
PRINT "That was first time round"
SLEEP 1                          'wait
CALL daftsub                     'multiplied by 2
PRINT "That was second time round"
SLEEP 1
CALL daftsub                     'by 3 this time
PRINT "That was third time round"
END
SUB daftsub
STATIC a%                        'value will be preserved
a% = a% + 1                      'increment it
PRINT N% * a%                    'print product
END  SUB                         'out
```

Associated with: COMMON, DIM, REDIM

Points to note:

Used in procedures before any use of local variables. Note that if you assign a value to the local variable this will ensure that it has this set value and not a value that has been carried over by the use of STATIC. Use STATIC when you want a variable to start at zero and be used with whatever value it gets in the subroutine next time. Typically you can increment it by whatever amount you like.

$STATIC

Type:	Metacommand
Typical syntax:	REM $STATIC
Action:	Makes all subsequently declared arrays of the static type, see Appendix B.
Options:	None.
Argument(s):	None.
Restrictions:	Must be preceded by REM or ' mark.

Example:

```
REM $STATIC
max% = 50
DIM names$(max%)   'this would normally be dynamic
```

Associated with: DIM, $DYNAMIC, REDIM, REM

Points to note:

$STATIC is really intended for compatibility with programs written for compiled BASIC (such as Turbo-BASIC). Static arrays can be obtained by using DIM along with a number. Dimensions declared using a variable, see example, are normally dynamic.

STEP

Type:	Statement
Typical syntax:	(a) FOR variable1 TO variable2 STEP number
	(b) graphics-statement STEP co-ordinates
Action:	In a FOR...NEXT loop, determines the increment used at the NEXT stage to alter the counter value.
	In graphics statements, STEP placed ahead of co-ordinate values makes all co-ordinates relative to the current cursor position.
Options:	None.
Argument(s):	In the FOR...NEXT loop, STEP can take any number, positive or negative, as an argument. In its graphics form, STEP takes no arguments.
Restrictions:	A step that is fractional will have no effect if the number variable is an integer the step number and the counter number should be of the same types.

Examples:

(a)
```
CLS
FOR n% = 10 TO 1 STEP -1        'count down
  PRINT n%; "seconds and counting"
  SLEEP 1                       'one second delay
  CLS
NEXT
PRINT "Blastoff!"
```

(b)
```
CLS
FOR n% = 1 TO 5                 'counting up
  PRINT n%
NEXT
PRINT "n% is now"; n%           'value is 6, one beyond end
FOR n% = 5 TO 1 STEP -1         'count down
  PRINT n%
NEXT
PRINT "n% is now"; n%           'value is 0, one step on
```

(c)
```
FOR n = 1 TO 5 STEP .01         'fractional step
  PRINT "Fractional"; n         'prints value of n
```

```
NEXT
REM Last number is 4.99002 - not a multiple of 0.01
REM because of cumulative imprecision of single-precision
REM numbers
```

(d)
```
SCREEN 12                  'VGA 640 x 480
CLS
CIRCLE (10, 10), 5         'draw one circle near top
FOR n% = 1 TO 45           'use loop
   CIRCLE STEP (10, 10), 5 'to draw more
NEXT
```

Associated with: CIRCLE, FOR...NEXT, GET, LINE, PAINT, PRESET, PSET, PUT

Points to note:

Example (b) shows that the value of the loop counter variable will always have been stepped beyond its end point at the end of a loop. The end point is determined by altering the counter by one step and comparing this with the end-value. This is important to remember if you are making use of the counter variable after the loop has finished.

Another point to note is the extent of the inaccuracy that can be caused by using a single-precision number variable in a FOR...NEXT count, as example (c) displays. For many purposes, this is unimportant but once again, if you were using the value of the count without rounding off it could cause problems.

Finally, (d) demonstrates the effect of using relative coordinates. Without the STEP statement, all the circles drawn in the loop would be in the same position as the first circle.

STICK

Type:	Function
Typical syntax:	variable = STICK(number)
Action:	Returns the X or Y coordinate of a selected joystick.
Options:	None.
Argument(s):	The number, placed between brackets, determines which coordinate for which joystick is returned:

0	x co-ordinate of joystick A.
1	y co-ordinate of joystick A.
2	x co-ordinate of joystick B.
3	y co-ordinate of joystick B.

Restrictions: The joysticks must be connected and working. STICK(0) *must be called* before any others are called (it triggers the recording of the other values).

Example:

```
DO WHILE INKEY$ = ""        'no key pressed
   LOCATE 20,5              'place cursor
   PRINT STICK (0)          'stick A x-value
   PRINT STICK (1)          'stick A y-value
   PRINT STICK (2)          'stick B x-value
LOOP
REM leave loop by pressing a key
```

Associated with: ON STRIG, STRIG function, STRIG statement

Points to note:

Useful mainly for games actions – but should you be writing a game in BASIC?

STOP

Type:	Statement
Typical syntax:	STOP
Action:	Halts program action and also suspends all trapping actions except for ON ERROR trapping.
Options:	None.
Argument(s):	None.
Restrictions:	The F5 key needs to be used to resume the program action.

Example:

```
DEFINT A Z
DIM gen$ (500)                        'array for data
CLS
n% = 1                                'counter
OPEN "serfile.dat" FOR INPUT AS #6    'open file
PRINT TAB(27); "DATA DISPLAY": PRINT
DO WHILE NOT EOF(6)                   'do until end
  INPUT #6, gen$(n%)                  'get data in array
  STOP                                'What is it?
LOOP                                  'continue
  CLOSE                               'close
  PRINT "End of file"
  END
  REM STOP line used in testing to check what has been
  REM read in from the file (using PRINT gen$(n%))
```

Associated with: END, SYSTEM

Points to note:

It would be unusual to include STOP permanently as part of a program, requiring the user to use the F5 key to continue. The more usual action is, as the example shows, to allow a program to be halted and variables printed (using the Immediate screen) so that you can see what is happening. The excellent debugging facilities of QBASIC make the use of STOP less important than it was in earlier versions of BASIC, and its use is now superseded by the action of inserting break points.

STR$

Type:	Function
Typical syntax:	string = STR$(number)
Action:	Converts a number in number format into a string, using as many characters as appear in the number when printed, plus 1 (see above).
Options:	None.
Argument(s):	The number used as an argument can be of any kind, enclosed in brackets.
Restrictions:	The string created by STR$ usually starts with a blank to allow spaces for a sign (+ or -).
Example:	

```
A# = 101463.2295
b$ = STR$(a#)
PRINT b$; " "; LEN(b$)
```

Associated with: VAL

Points to note:

LTRIM$ can be used to remove any unwanted leading spaces from a string form of number.

This conversion should not be confused with the LSET method. All numbers will be stored using a number of bytes that is determined by the number type rather then the number size, so that integers need two bytes, long integers and single-precision floats need four bytes, and double-precision floats need eight bytes. The string form needs one character per digit, one for a decimal point, plus one for a sign, so that, for example, the number:

21376.7704

which stored in eight bytes as a float needs 11 bytes as a string when STR$ is used. When LSET is used, only eight bytes are required, but printing the result gives meaningless garbage because of the coding that is used.

STRIG function

Type:	Function
Typical syntax:	variable = STRIG(number)
Action:	Returns the status of each joystick trigger as Boolean TRUE (-1) or FALSE (0).
Options:	None.
Argument(s):	The number, placed between brackets, is used to determine the joystick status, and for each number, the meaning of a TRUE return is as follows:

0	Lower joystick A trigger was pressed since last STRIG(0).
1	Lower joystick A trigger is currently being pressed.
2	Lower joystick B trigger was pressed since last STRIG(2).
3	Lower joystick B trigger is currently being pressed.
4	Upper joystick A trigger was pressed since last STRIG(4).
5	Upper joystick A trigger is currently being pressed.
6	Upper joystick B trigger was pressed since last STRIG(6).
7	Upper joystick B trigger is currently being pressed.

Restrictions: The joystick(s) must be connected, working and triggers enabled by using STRIG ON.

Examples:

```
STRIG (0) ON            'turn on event trapping
STRIG (2) ON
STRIG (4) ON
STRIG (6) ON
DO WHILE INKEY$ = " "
  PRINT STRIG (0)       'print status
  PRINT STRIG (1)
  PRINT STRIG (2)
  PRINT STRIG (3)
  PRINT STRIG (4)
  PRINT STRIG (5)
  PRINT STRIG (6)
  PRINT STRIG (7)
LOOP
END
```

Assiciated with: STICK, STRIG, ON STRIG Statements

Points to note: None.

STRIG statement

Type:	Statement
Typical syntax:	STRIG(number) ON
	STRIG(number) OFF
	STRIG(number) STOP
	ON STRING(number) GOSUB line
Action:	STRIG ON enables event trapping for the joystick trigger(s).
	STRIG OFF disables event trapping for the joystick trigger(s).
	STRIG STOP suspends event trapping for the joystick trigger(s).
	ON STRIG GOSUB defines a routine to run when a trigger is pressed.
Options:	None.
Argument(s):	The number argument, placed between brackets, determines the testing action:

0	Lower trigger, joystick A.
2	Lower trigger, joystick B.
4	Upper trigger, joystick A.
6	Upper trigger, joystick B.

Restrictions:	The joystick(s) must be connected and working.
Examples:	See under STRIG function.
Associated with:	STICK, STRIG function
Points to note:	
None.	

STRING$

Type:	Function returning string
Typical syntax:	variable = STRING$(number, character)
Action:	Returns a string made up of as many identical characters as is specified in the argument.
Options:	The character argument can be a literal such as "S" or an ASCII code for a character.
Argument(s):	The number of identical characters in the string and the character itself, separated by a comma and enclosed in brackets.
Restrictions:	STRING$ can make up a string of identical characters only, not a mixture of characters.

Example:

```
frame$ = STRING$(20, 223)          'shaded block
PRINT frame$ + HEADING + frame$
bar$ = STRING$(47, "-")
```

Associated with: SPACE$

Points to note:

The ability to use the ASCII code for the character allows the use of characters in the range 128 to 255.

SUB

Type:	Statement

Typical syntax:
SUB name   or   SUB name (parameters)
Statements   Statements
END SUB   END SUB

Action: Defines a procedure which can be called by name, placed anywhere in a program, and whose access is strictly controlled. All variables used in the procedure are local unless otherwise defined, and these variables can be defined as static.

Options: The word STATIC can be added to specify that local variables will retain values between calls to the SUB.

Argument(s): Each procedure must use a name which can take the standard QBASIC format, see Appendix G.

The parameters can consist of variable names, optionally, which can include a type, as in:

able AS INTEGER
Baker AS LONG
and so on.

Restrictions: A SUB must not start with a blank line, and the Editor will insert a REM if you attempt to type a blank line at the start of a SUB.

Examples:

(a)
```
DECLARE SUB demo2 ()          'put in by editor
DECLARE SUB demo ()           'also
CLS
DIM SHARED n%                 'global variable
n% = 10                       'assigned value
CALL demo                     'first SUB
PRINT "a% outside is"; a%     'no value
PRINT "b% outside is"; b%     'no value
END

SUB demo
a% = 2 * n%                   'n% is global
b% = 3 * n%
PRINT "a% inside demo is"; a% 'value 20
PRINT "b% inside demo is"; b% 'value 30
```

```
          CALL demo2
          END SUB

          SUB demo2
          PRINT "n% in demo2 is "; n%      'n% is global
          PRINT "a% in demo2 is "; a%      'no value
          PRINT "b% in demo2 is "; b%      'no value
          END SUB
(b)  DECLARE SUB demo2 (p%, q%)           '2 int. parameters
     DECLARE SUB demo (x%)                '1 int. parameter
     CLS
     n% = 10                             'local to main
     CALL demo(n%)                       'but passed to demo
     PRINT "a% outside is"; a%           'no value
     PRINT "b% outside is"; b%           'no value
     END

     SUB demo (x%)                       'value passed in
       a% = 2 * x%                       'and used
       b% = 3 * x%                       'twice
       PRINT "a% inside demo is"; a%     'gives 20
       PRINT "b% inside demo is"; b%     'gives 30
       CALL demo2(a%, b%)                'pass to another
     END SUB

     SUB demo2 (p%, q%)                  '2 parameters
       PRINT "n% in demo2 is "; n%       'no value
       PRINT "p% in demo2 is "; p%       'passed in
       PRINT "q% in demo2 is "; q%       'passed in
     END SUB
```

Associated with: CALL, DECLARE, FUNCTION

Points to note:

A procedure named Myproc can be called either by using CALL Myproc or, more simply by using Myproc. Parameters able and Baker would be used in the form:

> CALL Myproc (able, Baker)   OR
>
> Myproc able, Baker

In the second format, enclosing a parameter name in brackets will ensure that the procedure does *not* alter the value of that parameter. Any parameter in the parameter list can be used to pass in data or to pass data out, and by using the no-bracket option, the parameter can be treated as if its value inside the procedure is local.

SWAP

Type:	Statement
Typical syntax:	SWAP variable1, variable2
Action:	Interchanges the values of two variables. Used mainly in sorting routines.
Options:	None.
Argument(s):	Two variable names of the same type separated by a comma.
Restrictions:	Variables must be of identical type.

Example:

```
CLS
DIM j%(100)                       'array of integers
FOR n% = 1 TO 100                 'fill with random
  j%(n%) = RND * 100              'integers
NEXT
PRINT "Sorting now"               'simple bubble-sort
DO 'start
  p% = 0                          'marker for no swap
  FOR x% = 1 TO 99                'number to check
    IF j%(x%) > j%(x% + 1) THEN   'test which larger
      SWAP j%(x%), j%(x% + 1)     'swap if needed
      p% = 1                      'and mark swap
    END IF
  NEXT                            'next one
LOOP UNTIL p% = 0                 'no swaps marker
FOR n% = 1 TO 100                 'now
PRINT j%(n%); " ";                'print the list
NEXT                              '- that's it
```

Associated with: None

Points to note:

Used in sort routines, as example. Versions of BASIC with no SWAP statement have to use lines such as:

```
temp% = j%(x%)
j%(x%) = j%(x% + 1)
j%(x% + 1) = temp%
```

and if you find such lines in a program, you can replace them by the single line:

```
SWAP j%(x%), j%(x% + 1)
```

SYSTEM

Type:	Statement
Typical syntax:	SYSTEM
Action:	Closes all open files and returns to QBASIC.
Options:	None.
Argument(s):	None.
Restrictions:	None.
Example:	

```
SLEEP 2 NEXT
PRINT "Now leaving program"
SLEEP 1
SYSTEM
```

Associated with: END

Points to note:

SYSTEM is included in QBASIC more for compatibility with older BASIC versions than for current use. In compiled BASIC programs it provides for a return to MS-DOS, but in QBASIC it does no more than END would do. It does not, as you might expect, return to MS-DOS. To return to MS-DOS temporarily, use SHELL.

TAB

Type:	Function
Typical syntax:	PRINT TAB(number); item
	PRINT TAB(number);item; TAB(number);item...
Action:	Starts printing on a specified column.
Options:	None.
Argument(s):	An integer column number, using 0 or 1 to 80, within brackets.
Restrictions:	Arguments 0 and 1 have the same effect. Arguments greater than the permitted column number have the same effect as using number MOD column, see example (b).

Examples:

(a)
```
CLS
PRINT TAB(1)"L"; TAB(80)"R"        'left and right sides
PRINT TAB(37); "CENTRE"            'central position
PRINT TAB(5); "Start here..."      'indented text
```

(b)
```
CLS
PRINT "Top line"
PRINT TAB(2); "A"
PRINT TAB(5) "TAB(5); ";TAB(3 * 80 + 5); "Where is this?"
REM TAB(3 * 80 + 5) has the same effect as TAB(5)
```

Associated with: LOCATE, LPRINT, PRINT, PRINT #, PRINT USING, SPC

Points to note:

TAB is the most commonly used method of arranging text along a line of print, but when a PRINT instruction contains a set of TABs the position numbers must be arranged in order. If you need to be able to print at random positions on the screen use LOCATE.

TAN

Type:	Function returning double-precision number
Typical syntax:	variable = TAN(angle)
Action:	Returns the tangent (see Appendix A) of the angle (in radian units) used as the argument, enclosed in brackets.
Options:	None.
Argument(s):	The angle in radians for which the tangent value is needed, as a number, variable or expression, placed between brackets.
Restrictions:	Values of angle close to 0 and to multiples of PI/2 (90°) are unreliable.

Example:

```
CONST PI = 3.1416            'for conversion
Horizont = 22.67            'distance
deg = 27                    'angle in degrees
angle = 27 * PI/180         'convert
Vert = Horizont * TAN(angle)  'calculate vertical
PRINT "Vert = "; Vert       ' gives 11.55097
REM Pocket calculator gives 11.550941
REM difference due to using approximation
REM for value of PI
```

Associated with: ATN, COS, SIN

Points to note:

To convert angle in degrees into radians, multiply angle in degrees by PI and divide by 180. This can be done by creating a defined function for the purpose. Use a PI value of 15 figures if you need double-precision accuracy.

THEN

Type:	Statement
Typical syntax:	IF condition THEN action

IF condition THEN
   Statements
END IF

IF condition THEN
   Statements
   ELSE IF
      Statements
END IF

Action: Defines the action(s) to be carried out when the condition test that follows IF returns TRUE.

Options: ELSE can be used without a following IF to define actions that will be carried out when the condition returns FALSE.

Argument(s): None.

Restrictions: Can be used only in conjunction with IF.

Examples:

(a)
```
IF Age => 35 THEN GOSUB Middle
```

(b)
```
IF Dist <= 100 THEN
    AVsp = 45
    GOSUB calctime
END IF
```

Associated with: ELSE, ON...GOSUB, ON...GOTO, SELECT CASE

Points to note:
Large constructions using IF, ELSE IF and ELSE are difficult to plan and to read. It is often much easier to use SELECT CASE.

TIME$ function

Type:	Function returning string
Typical syntax:	variable = TIME$
Action:	Returns a string variable of the current time read from the computer's clock system.
Options:	None.
Argument(s):	None.
Restrictions:	The returned string is of fixed length, eight bytes, padded out if necessary. The 24-hour clock (military time) system is used. The accuracy of TIME$ depends on the accuracy of the computer's clock system, see Notes.
Action:	Returns a string variable of the current time read from the computer's clock system.

Example:

```
PRINT TIME$         'format is hh:mm:ss
T$ = TIME$          'assigned
```

Associated with: TIMER, TIME$ statement

Points to note:

The time setting can be altered by using the TIME$ statement. The timekeeping of the computer's clock system is notoriously poor, despite the use of a quartz crystal. This is because of interruptions to the system which result in hiccups in the timing. If the use of TIME$ function is important, reset the clock daily (the TIME$ statement can be used).

TIME$ statement

Type: Statement

Typical syntax: TIME$ = timestring

Action: Sets the system clock to a time defined by the supplied string.

Options: None.

Argument(s):   None.

Restrictions: The time string can consist of hh, hh:mm or hh:mm:ss depending the precision of setting that is required. The figures can be used within quotes, such as "10:22:35", and a colon is used as a separator.

Examples:

(a)
```
TIME$ = "11:24:50"
```

(b)
```
set$ = "12:00:00"                  'prepare for check
TIME$ = set$                       'run this at mid-day
```

(c)
```
PRINT TIME$                        'check
h% = VAL(LEFT$(TIME$, 2))          'get hour number
m% = VAL(MID$(TIME$, 4, 2))        'minute
s% = VAL(RIGHT$(TIME$, 2))         'second
h% = h% + 1                        'advance hour
h$ = LTRIM$(STR$(h%))              'back to string
m$ = LTRIM$(STR$(m%))              'minutes
s$ = LTRIM$(STR$(s%))              'seconds
TIME$ = h$ + ":" + m$ + ":" + s$   'into TIMER$
PRINT TIME$                        'check
REM Advances TIMER$ for Summer time
REM Use h% = h% -1 for Winter.
```

Associated with: DATE$, TIME$ function

Points to note:

A change in the time setting remains in force until it is changed again. It does not revert when you exit from QBASIC

TIMER function

Type: Function

Typical syntax: variable = TIMER

Action: Returns the number of seconds since midnight.

Options: None.

Argument(s): None.

Restrictions: Depends on the precision of the system clock, which can be very poor.

Examples:

```
IF TIMER <= 25200 THEN
   GOSUB Earlymorn    'runs only before 7.00 a.m.
END IF

RANDOMIZE TIMER       'make random numbers more random
```

Associated with: ON TIMER, RANDOMIZE, TIMER statement, TIME$

Points to note:

If TIMER is assigned to any other variable, a long integer should be used because the value of TIMER can exceed the short integer range.

TIMER statement

Type: Statement

Typical syntax: TIMER ON
TIMER OFF
TIMER STOP
ON TIMER(number) GOSUB line

Action: ON TIMER provides a routine which is activated at regular intervals as determined by the argument. This is typically used to print a time on the screen which will be updated each second or each minute.

Options: ON enables TIMER trapping.

OFF disables TIMER trapping.

STOP suspends TIMER trapping. TIMER event that occurs while STOP is in use will be detected only when TIMER ON is used later.

Argument(s): The number used in ON TIMER will determine the number of seconds between calls to the subroutine. The permitted range is 1 to 86,400.

Restrictions: Trapping is not activated until the TIMER ON statement has been used.

Examples:

```
CLS
ON TIMER(10) GOSUB looktime    'set up routine, 10 seconds
TIMER ON                       'activate
PRINT
FOR n% = 1 TO 100              'slow loop which will
   PRINT "Count is "; n%       'run while timer
   FOR j = 1 TO 3000: NEXT     'works
NEXT
END

looktime:                      'timer routine
col% = POS(0)                  'save the cursor col
row% = CSRLIN                  'and row positions
LOCATE 1, 70                   'place for time print
PRINT TIME$                    'print it here
```

```
     LOCATE row%, col%              'cursor back in place
     RETURN                        'back to work
```

Associated with: TIMER function

Points to note:

When the subroutine called by the TIMER trap runs, further timer interrupts are turned off until the RETURN statement is met. Using a TIMER OFF statement in the subroutine will prevent the timer trapping from being resumed after the first call.

TROFF

Type:	Statement
Typical syntax:	TROFF
Action:	Turns off the tracing of program statements that was started by using TRON. TROFF can be placed into a program line at a point further into the program than TRON, so that the statements between TRON and TROFF are run slowly, with each statement printed out.
Options:	None.
Argument(s):	None.
Restrictions:	Used only following a TRON statement. Obsolescent statement.
Examples:	

```
TRON
FOR X% = 1 TO 6
PRINT "Line number ";X%
NEXT
TROFF
PRINT "End of test"
```

Assiciated with: TRON

Points to note:

TRON and TROFF are compatible with statements in older BASIC versions but are not required in QBASIC because the Editor can be used to control tracing.

TRON

Type:	Statement
Typical syntax:	TRON
Action:	Turns on tracing, so that each statement is printed as it is executed. In older versions of BASIC, each line number was printed to indicate that the line had been executed.
Options:	None.
Argument(s):	None.
Restrictions:	Obsolescent, use for compatibility only.
Examples:	See entry for TROFF.
Assiciated with:	TROFF

Points to note:

TRON and TROFF are compatible with statements in older BASIC versions but are not required in QBASIC because the Editor can be used to control tracing.

TYPE

Type:	Statement
Typical syntax:	TYPE name
	element AS type
	element AS type
	....
	END TYPE
Action:	Allows a new variable type to be created, consisting of elements of established types (integer, long integer, short, single, double, string) or a previously defined new type. Variables of this type can then be declared.
Options:	None.
Argument(s):	A defined variable type must be named, using the normal QBASIC convention on names, see App. G.
Restrictions:	Any type used in a definition must be of an established type or a user-defined type that has previously been declared in an earlier TYPE statement.

Examples:

```
TYPE Record                'name of type
   Name AS STRING * 20      'fixed length string
   Cash AS SINGLE          'and single float
END TYPE                   'end of definition

DIM Debtor AS Record       'variable of type Record
Debtor.Name = "Mattheson"  'name part
Debtor.Cash = 24.56`       'cash part
```

Associated with: COMMON, DIM, REDIM, SHARED, STATIC

Points to note:

A user-defined variable type can be used in a definition along with DIM, REDIM, COMMON, STATIC, or SHARED to create the required variable.

Note that the use of a defined TYPE replaces the need for FIELD, LSET, and RSET in random-access filing. A type can be declared, using whatever combination of other variables (or even other declared types) is needed. The example shows how parts of a type are referred to as variables, using a multi-part name with parts separated by a dot. If your user-defined type itself contained another user-defined type, the name of a portion would require three parts separated by two dots.

UBOUND

Type:	Function returning integer or long integer
Typical syntax:	variable = UBOUND(array, dimension)
Action:	Returns the upper limit of the subscript for an array, the largest subscript number that can be used.
Options:	None.
Argument(s):	Array name and number of dimension, default 1, separated by a comma and enclosed in brackets.
Restrictions:	None.

Examples:

(a)
```
DIM Intarray(100)          'dimension array
..............             'other statements
PRINT UBOUND(Intarray,1)   'Gives 100
```

(b)
```
DIM matrix(20,5,10)        'dimension 3D array
..............            'other statements
PRINT UBOUND (matrix, 2)   'gives 5
```

Associated with: DIM, REDIM, LBOUND, OPTION BASE

Points to note:

For an array of more than one dimension, such as Cubit (a%,b%,c%) the dimension number 1, 2, or 3 must be used to find the upper limit for each dimension separately.

You would normally know the dimensions of an array used in a program, and the purpose of UBOUND is to read the dimensions of an array that was not dimensioned by you or has been redimensioned using variables whose values you could not know with certainty. Values read from a file, with the count number used to dimension or redimension a dynamic array, come into this category.

UCASE$

Type:	Function returning string
Typical syntax:	variable = UCASE$(string)
Action:	Returns a string of upper-case characters corresponding to lower-case or mixed lower and upper-case characters in the argument.
Options:	None.
Argument(s):	A string containing lower-case characters, in brackets.
Restrictions:	A Type Mismatch error occurs if the argument is not a string.

Example:

```
PRINT UCASE$("shotley Marina")  'prints SHOTLEY MARINA
A$ = UCASE$(A$)                 'convert A$ to upper-case
```

Associated with: LCASE$

Points to note:

The ASCII code range uses numbers 64 to 90 for A to Z, and 97 to 122 for a to z, so that, for example, Z is arranged in a sort action before a. String comparisons should therefore be made using UCASE$ to avoid incorrect ordering of upper and lower case, using lines such as:

```
IF UCASE$(A$) < UCASE$(J$) THEN SWAP A$,J$
```

If the argument is a null string, then the returned string is also null. If the argument is a number in string form it is unaffected.

UNLOCK

Type:	Statement
Typical syntax:	UNLOCK filenumber
	UNLOCK filenumber, record
	UNLOCK filenumber, start TO end
Action:	Unlocks a networked file. Sequential files are totally unlocked, random-access and binary files can be partially unlocked, selecting individual records or bytes or a range.
Options:	A single record or byte can be unlocked, or a range of records or bytes.
Argument(s):	The filenumber is the number used in the OPEN statement, with or without the hash sign. For a single unit, the record number can be used for a random access file to unlock one record, or a byte number can be used to unlock a single byte of a binary file. A range of records or bytes can be unlocked by using the start and end numbers.
Restrictions:	Applies to networked files only. UNLOCK used on a sequential file unlocks the whole file, and the record and range numbers are ignored.

Example:

```
OPEN "ranfile" FOR RANDOM AS #1      'open file
UNLOCK #1, 1 TO 1000                 'unlock 1000 records
```

Associated with: LOCK

Points to note:

The LOCK and UNLOCK statements should be used only for networked files, and only if you have a clear understanding of the networking system.

UNTIL

Type:	Statement
Typical syntax:	DO UNTIL condition
	Statements
	LOOP
	DO
	Statements
	LOOP UNTIL condition
Action:	Forms the condition for a loop ending or not starting, depending on the position of UNTIL.
Options:	Can be used following DO or following LOOP.
Argument(s):	A test condition which can be TRUE or FALSE.
Restrictions:	Used only as illustrated in a DO...LOOP construction.

Examples:

(a)
```
total = 0                         'initialise
j = 1                             'variables
CLS
PRINT "Enter numbers for totalling; 0 to end"
DO UNTIL j = 0                    'j is already set
INPUT j                           'new value
total = total + j                 'add in
PRINT "Total so far is"; total    'print it
LOOP                              'back to DO
PRINT "End of entry"              'end
```

(b)
```
total = 0                         'initialise
CLS
PRINT "Enter numbers for totalling; 0 to end"
DO                                'start loop
INPUT j                           'get number
total = total + j                 'add in
PRINT "Total so far is"; total    'print
LOOP UNTIL j = 0                  'end condition
PRINT "End of entry"              'end
```

(c)
```
CLS
DO WHILE a$ <> "X"      'end condition after read and loop
READ a$                 'action follows test condition
IF a$ = "X" THEN EXIT DO      'avoids printing X
PRINT a$                      'print name
LOOP                          loop back
DATA Glenfiddich, Glenmorangie, Laphroaig
DATA Islay Mist, Talisker, X
```

Associated with: DO, EXIT, LOOP, WHILE

Points to note:

The position of UNTIL determines the point of testing for the end of the loop, so that if UNTIL follows DO, the loop is tested at the start and will not run if the test condition returns TRUE. If UNTIL is used at the end of the loop, the loop will run at least once, even if the test condition returns TRUE.

EXIT DO can be used to end the loop at some point other than the start or the end. In the third example, using EXIT ensures that the terminating value of X is not printed. The loop will read this value, print it and then end on the next test in the DO line. By using EXIT, the loop is terminated whenever the X item is read. Using EXIT in this way avoids the need to test in the DO line, and the test has been shown only because it is often retained (belt and braces programming) or because another test (such as for a maximum number of items) can be used in the DO line.

VAL

Type:	Function returning number
Typical syntax:	numbervariable = VAL(string)
Action:	Returns in number form numerals that are in string form.
Options:	None.
Argument(s):	A string, enclosed in brackets, consisting of numerals created from a string assignment or using a string literal such as "123".
Restrictions:	Any numbers following a letter other than D, E &H or &O will be ignored. You can use VAL ("123ABC") to return 123, but VAL("ABC123") will return 0. Valid number characters are 0 to 9, +, -, decimal point, letters E and D.

Example:

```
answer$ = "1456ABC22      'string assigned
num = VAL (answer$)        'value taken
PRINT num                  'prints 1456
```

Associated with: LTRIM$, RTRIM$, STR$

Points to note:

Functions LTRIM$ and RTRIM$ can be used to remove unwanted spaces such as can be created by using STR$.

VAL is used along with string input to allow the user to type data which can be number or string, with conversions done later. This avoids the use of input to a number variable which always carries the risk of an input like 22Z causing a *Redo from Start* error message.

You can use VAL to convert hexadecimal and octal numbers into ordinary denary form, provided that the octal or hex numbers are in string form and use the distinguishing &O and &H prefixes respectively. For example:

```
PRINT VAL("&HFFFF")        'gives -1
PRINT VAL("&O772")         'gives 506
```

VARPTR

Type:	Function
Typical syntax:	variable = VARPTR(var)
Action:	Returns the memory address for a variable in the current data segment.
Options:	None.
Argument(s):	The variable var is any variable type, including a user-defined type, held between brackets.
Restrictions:	The current data segment, as set by DEF SEG, will be used.

Example:

```
A% = 280
PRINT VARPTR(A%)
Name$ = "Sinclair"
X% = VARPTR(Name$)
```

Associated with: CALL ABSOLUTE, DEF SEG, PEEK, POKE, VARPTR$, VARSEG

Points to note:

The address that VARPTR returns is referred to as an offset address, meaning that it is relative to the start of the 64K segment of memory that is currently in use for data, or has been selected by using DEF SEG. VARPTR returns the first address number, and the contents can be found by using a loop incorporating PEEK. Contents of memory can be altered by using a POKE loop.

When VARPTR is applied to a number variable, it gives the location of the first of the bytes that make up the number. When VARPTR is used on a string variable, it yields the length of the string and the memory address numbers, not the string itself. This is a way of allowing predictable handling of variables, because it allows the details of any string to be stored in four bytes. The system used for storing a number also ensures a predictable number of bytes for each variable value.

See Appendix C for details of the segmented addressing of the PC machines.

VARPTR$

Type:	Function
Typical syntax:	string = VARPTR$(var)
Action:	Returns the address of a variable as a string for use in PLAY or DRAW strings. The variable is usually a string variable used for another DRAW or PLAY string, so that a form of DRAW or PLAY subroutine can be used.
Options:	None.
Argument(s):	The name of any variable type, including a user-defined variable, between brackets.
Restrictions:	Used only along with PLAY and DRAW statements to specify a string address for use with the 'X' sub-command.

Example:

```
SCREEN 12                          'VGA 640 x 480
COLOR 0
CLS
SB$ = "u100r20d100r20"             'minor part
XS$ = ""                           'clear
FOR N% = 1 TO 5
XS$ = XS$ + SB$                    'build up set
NEXT
GR$ = "bm20,180;c14X" + VARPTR$(XS$)  'add in sub-string
DRAW GR$                           'draw it
```

Associated with: DRAW, PLAY

Points to note:

This function is provided only for the PLAY and DRAW actions. Earlier versions of interpreted BASIC that used PLAY and DRAW could follow the 'X' subcommand with the name of a string variable directly. Compiled BASIC versions required the VARPTR$ format, and QBASIC has been brought into line with the compiled versions. Watch for the use of 'X' in DRAW and PLAY strings in older programs in which VARPTR$ did not need to be used.

VARSEG

Type:	Function
Typical syntax:	variable = VARSEG(var)
Action:	Returns the segment address of a variable, using numbers in the range 0 to 65535.
Options:	None.
Argument(s):	The name of any variable type, including a user-defined type or an element of an array.
Restrictions:	None.

Example:

```
X% = 25                           'variable assigned
DEF SEG = VARSEG(X%)              'establish data segment
loc% = VARPTR(X%)                 'find address
PRINT PEEK (loc%);PEEK(loc% + 1)  'print stored values
```

Associated with: CALL ABSOLUTE, DEF SEG, PEEK, POKE, VARPTR, VARPTR$

Points to note:

See Appendix C for the segmented addressing methods of the PC type of machine. VARSEG is used to find the segment number that is associated with the VARPTR number for the location of a variable. All scalar variables (non-array variables) are located in the same data segment, so that once the segment number for one scalar variable has been found the same number can be used for all the others. Use VARSEG to find the number to use along with DEF SEG preceding PEEK and POKE actions.

VIEW

Type:	Statement
Typical syntax:	VIEW (topleft) - (bottomright)
	VIEW (topleft) - (bottomright), colour
	VIEW (topleft) - (bottomright), colour, border
Action:	Creates a *graphics* window (a viewport) which can be used independently of others and independently of the main screen
Options:	The word SCREEN can be used immediately following VIEW to make the co-ordinates used in other statements relative to the whole screen rather than to the window. With SCREEN omitted, for example, using SET 20,50 will set a pixel at these co-ordinates relative to the top lefthand corner of the window, not relative to the top lefthand corner of the screen.
Argument(s):	X and Y co-ordinates for the top lefthand corner and the bottom righthand corner of the window (viewport). If no arguments are used, the whole screen is taken to be the window. The optional arguments are a colour number for the colour that fills the rectangular window area, and a border colour for the frame. Co-ordinates are enclosed in brackets.
Restrictions:	Applies only to *graphics* screen windows. The range of arguments depends on the values used in the SCREEN statement. Pixels that fall outside the VIEW area cannot be SET or RESET. Using SCREEN cancels any windows established by a previous use of VIEW. Using CLS will clear only the current VIEW.

Examples:

```
(a) SCREEN 12                             'VGA screen
    CLS                                   'clear
    VIEW SCREEN (100, 100)-(1, 1), , 15   'first window
    CIRCLE (50, 50), 20                   'draw
    VIEW SCREEN (300, 300)-(150, 150), , 15  'second window
    LINE (160, 160)-(220, 220), , B       'draw
    REM SCREEN must be used before VIEW
    REM Co-ordinates are full-screen values
```

(b)
```
CLS
SCREEN 12                       'VGA screen
VIEW (1, 1)-(100, 100), , 15    '1st. window
CIRCLE (50, 50), 15             'relative co-ordinates
VIEW (200, 200)-(400, 400), , 15 '2nd. window
LINE (10, 10)-(180, 180), , B   'draw box
REM co-ordinates are relative to top left-hand
REM corner of the window.
```

Associated with: CLS, SCREEN, VIEW PRINT, WINDOW

Points to note:

VIEW is used to create a graphics screen box, whose height and width can be of any size up to the maximum size of the screen. The VIEW PRINT statement is used to create a text window, which must be of full screen width. Note that the WINDOW statement establishes the co-ordinate system for use in a window (including a full screen) so that instead of using co-ordinates 0 to 640 and 0 to 200 you could use 0 to 1000 for each direction, or whatever units you wanted to use.

Remember the use of CLS along with a number to clear text and graphics windows selectively.

VIEW PRINT

Type:	Statement
Typical syntax:	VIEW PRINT toprow TO bottomrow
Action:	Creates a *text* window of a defined number of rows and of fixed full width.
Options:	None.
Argument(s):	Top row number and bottom row number. If these are omitted the whole screen will be used.
Restrictions:	Creates a window (viewport) for the text screen only. Each text window is the width of the full screen (unlike a graphics window).

Example:

```
CLS                              ' whole screen
PRINT "This is a title line which will not scroll"
VIEW PRINT 12 TO 24              'bottom half
PRINT "This is where scrolling takes place"
FOR n% = 1 TO 2000              'start writing
PRINT "A";                       'fill with A
SLEEP 0.1                        'wait
NEXT
PRINT "End of scrolling"
SLEEP 2                          'wait
CLS                              'clear window only
END
```

Associated with: CLS, LOCATE, PRINT, LPRINT, SCREEN, WIDTH

Points to note:

The window created in this way can be cleared, scrolled and printed independently of any other part of the screen. Remember the use of CLS with a number 0 to 2 to use with such windows.

WAIT

Type:	Statement
Typical syntax:	WAIT port, AND expression1
	WAIT port, AND expression1, XOR expression2
Action:	Suspends program actions until some preset bit pattern is read from a port.
Options:	None.
Argument(s):	The port address must be specified (usually in hexadecimal). The first expression will be ANDed with the byte read from the port, and if the result is not zero, the wait action ends. The second expression can optionally be XORed with the byte from the port *before* the AND action is carried out.
Restrictions:	Port address must be valid. Some care is needed to provide a combination of XOR and AND that will provide a zero for unwanted inputs and any number for wanted inputs.
Example:	

```
CLS
PRINT "Press Pause key to end"
WAIT &H60, 64
PRINT "Input received"
END
REM Safer to re-start after this!
```

Associated with: INP, OUT

Points to note:

Use of this statement requires some knowledge of machine code and the design of the PC type of machine. Some actions that might use WAIT are much easier to carry out using other statements. For example, the use of the keyboard port at &H60 along with WAIT is a very clumsy method compared with using a PEEK of the &H417 and &H418 addresses.

Beware of using old BASIC programs that contain WAIT commands used for a pause (equivalent to SLEEP in QBASIC) as these could cause mayhem on the computer if they mis-used a port address.

WEND

Type:	Statement
Typical syntax:	WEND
Action:	Ends a loop started with WHILE.
Options:	None.
Argument(s):	None.
Restrictions:	Used only to end the WHILE form of loop. WEND used without WHILE generates Error 30. EXIT cannot be used in the WHILE...WEND loop.

Example:

```
WHILE count% =<56
GOSUB checkitem
WEND
```

Associated with: DO, FOR, LOOP, NEXT

Points to note:

WHILE...WEND is included in QBASIC mainly for compatibility with other versions of BASIC (including Locomotive) rather than for use in new programs. The DO...LOOP construction is much more flexible and should be used in new programs.

WHILE

Type:	Statement
Typical syntax:	WHILE condition
	Statements
	WEND

Action: Carries out loop actions for as long as the condition returns TRUE. The end of the loop is marked by WEND. This is equivalent to:

DO WHILE condition
   statements
LOOP

Options: None.

Argument(s): Any condition that can return Boolean TRUE or FALSE.

Restrictions: The loop must be terminated with WEND. Note that using WHILE -1 will cause the loop to be endless. WHILE without WEND generates Error 29. There is no EXIT provision for a WHILE...WEND loop, making the DO WHILE...LOOP version preferable.

Example:

```
DIM file$(1 TO 100)              'prepare array
j% = 1                          'initialise
nam$ = "dummy"                  'allow loop
WHILE UCASE$(nam$) <> "END"     'to run
PRINT "Enter name (type END to end)"
INPUT nam$                      'value
file$(j%) = nam$                'to array
j% = j% + 1                     'increment
IF j% => 101 THEN EXIT WHILE    'test for limit
WEND                            'more
```

Associated with: DO, FOR, LOOP, NEXT, WEND

Points to note:
WHILE...WEND is included in QBASIC mainly for compatibility with other versions of BASIC (such as Locomotive) rather than for use in new programs. The DO...LOOP construction is more flexible.

A common fault in a WHILE...WEND loop is that the loop does not run, because whatever is tested in the first line returns FALSE. For example, using:

```
WHILE num <> 0
INPUT num
total = total + num
WEND
PRINT "Total is ";total
END
```

will result in a loop that does not run, because the default of QBASIC is that a variable which has not been assigned has a zero or null value. Since the loop starts with nothing assigned to num, this is equivalent to starting with num = 0. and the loop cannot run. The solution in this case is to assign a dummy value, perhaps num = 1 just ahead of the WHILE line. This is an example of the type of problem which makes the the DO...LOOP construction preferable.

WIDTH

Type:	Statement
Typical syntax:	WIDTH
	WIDTH col,row
	WIDTH filenumber, col
	WIDTH device, col
	WIDTH LPRINT col

Action: Specifies the width of lines sent to a file, a device or a printer. Can also be used to specify the text screen to be used in terms of columns and rows selected from a restricted set.

Options: Can be used to control screen printing, width of text sent to a file or to another device, or to a printer.

Argument(s): Column and row numbers for the whole-screen display, using the permitted values of 40 or 80 for columns and 25, 30, 43, 50, or 60 for rows. Where a file, device or printer is the subject of the WIDTH statement, the column width only can be specified as 40 or 80 or higher numbers, typically 132. For a file, the filenumber as used in the OPEN statement must be used.

Restrictions: Low-resolution graphics cards will not allow the higher row numbers to be used.

Examples:

```
SCREEN 0                                'text
WIDTH 40                                'low resolution
PRINT "Large letters"
SLEEP 1                                 'wait
WIDTH 80                                'high resolution
PRINT "Smaller letters"
SLEEP 1
WIDTH "LPT1",132                        'wide printing
REM Use this only if you can set your printer
REM to 15 or 17 characters per inch (condensed)
```

Associated with: LPRINT, PRINT, SCREEN, VIEW PRINT

Points to note:
Device strings can include SCRN: , COM1:, COM2:, LPT1:, LPT2:, LPT3:. All of these device names must be enclosed in quotes.

WINDOW

Type:	Statement
Typical syntax:	WINDOW
	WINDOW (topleft) (bottomright)
Action:	Defines the co-ordinates that can be used for the whole screen or in a window, which need not be the same as the conventional 0, 639 and 0, 479 coordinates used for the whole screen. Following a WINDOW statement, the new co-ordinates must be used for all statements that require co-ordinates.
Options:	The word SCREEN can be added immediately following WINDOW to specify that Y co-ordinates are the *normal* non-Cartesian type used by QBASIC. This means that Y=0 is at the top and the maximum value of Y is at the bottom, the reverse of the normal graph arrangement. Omitting SCREEN makes the co-ordinate system take ascending Y values as meaning a movement from bottom to top of the screen.
Argument(s):	Co-ordinates of top lefthand corner and bottom righthand corner of the window. Using WINDOW with no arguments returns to normal screen co-ordinates. The co-ordinate numbers must be enclosed in brackets.
Restrictions:	Use with graphics windows only
Example:	

```
SCREEN 12
CLS
GOSUB drawit
SLEEP 2
WINDOW (0,0) - (2559, 1919)
GOSUB drawit
SLEEP 2
WINDOW
END
drawit:
CIRCLE (300, 200), 100
RETURN
```

Associated with: CLS, PMAP, POINT, SCREEN, VIEW

Points to note:

Use PMAP to convert between co-ordinates as defined by WINDOW and the normal whole-screen co-ordinates. Note that defining new co-ordinates of, for example, 0 to 5000 in each direction does not means that the screen display now has 5000 x 5000 pixels it is still the same screen of (for VGA) 640 x 480 pixels. The WINDOW action simply allows a greater range of numbers to be used.

This allows, for example, graphics programs written for the full screen, to be used in a small window, by defining the WINDOW as using the same co-ordinate range. In this way, a graphics subroutine can be used in any size of window. You can also make use of a co-ordinate set for another computer.

WRITE

Type: Statement

Typical syntax: WRITE data

      WRITE filenumber, data

Action: Sends data to the screen or to a sequential file, which must be open.

Options: WRITE can be used either to the screen or to a file (including a device file such as PRN:).

Argument(s): The data can be arranged as for PRINT, with items separated by commas. For writing to a file, the filenumber is the number used in the OPEN statement, with or without the hash sign.

Restrictions: There is no space placed ahead of a positive number.

Example:

```
CLS
FOR j% = 1 TO 4
   READ nam$, num%          'read items
   PRINT nam$, num%         'print
   WRITE nam$, num%         'write note difference
NEXT
DATA "This",12,"IS",13,"PRINT",14,"WRITE"15
REM Note effect of comma on WRITE
```

Associated with: INPUT, LINE INPUT, OPEN, PRINT, LPRINT

Points to note:

When you use WRITE it will insert commas between items and place quotation marks around strings as they are written. Data placed into a sequential file by WRITE can be read by the INPUT statement. This makes WRITE # preferable to PRINT # for file use, whereas PRINT is normally preferable to WRITE for using with the screen or the printer.

The example shows that the statement WRITE a,b will write the comma literally, not use it as a 14-zone separator as PRINT does.

XOR

Type: Function returning Boolean TRUE or FALSE

Typical syntax: expression1 XOR expression2

Action: Returns a Boolean TRUE or FALSE depending on the returns from the two expressions:

Expression 1	Expression 2	Result of XOR
FALSE	FALSE	FALSE
FALSE	TRUE	TRUE
TRUE	FALSE	TRUE
TRUE	TRUE	FALSE

This is the normal meaning of OR as one or the other but not both, asdistinct from the Boolean OR operator which includes both.

Options: None.

Argument(s): Two expressions which each return a Boolean TRUE or FALSE, one placed ahead of XOR, the other following.

Restrictions: Avoid using with numbers unless you understand binary code and the effects of bitwise actions.

Example:

```
A% = 9                  'binary 1001
PRINT A% XOR 1          ' 1001 XOR 0001
REM result is binary 1110, which is 14
```

Associated with: AND, EQV, IMP, NOT, OR

Points to note:

Using XOR with numbers can produce unexpected results because each bit of the binary representation of each number is XORed with the corresponding bit of the other number. For example, 8 XOR 7 returns with 15, but 9 XOR 13 returns with 4.

A number XORed with itself returns zero. When a number is XORed with a second number, the XOR of the result, using the second number again, is the first number. For example, 5 XOR 7 gives 2, and 2 XOR 7 gives 5 again. This is often used as a coding and decoding action.

The EQV function performs the opposite of the XOR action by returning TRUE if the expressions are both true and FALSE otherwise.

Appendix A: Angles and trigonometrical ratios

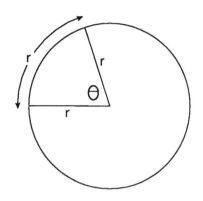

Figure A1.

Angle is 1 radian if the arc distance equals the radius.

For any distance l along the rim,
l= r.θ
where θ is the angle.

The natural unit of angle is the radian, which is defined as shown in Figure A1 above. For any arc of a circle, the angle at the centre of the arc is given in radians by the arc length divided by the radius. This can be rearranged to the form:

arc length = radius x angle

The trigonometrical ratios are defined for a triangle with one right angle as shown below.

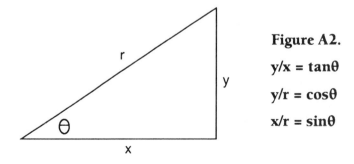

Figure A2.

$y/x = \tan\theta$

$y/r = \cos\theta$

$x/r = \sin\theta$

The longest side of such a triangle is always the hypotenuse, the side opposite the right angle. The sine and cosine of an angle are ratios of lengths of one of the sides that make up the angle to the hypotenuse. The tangent is the ratio of the sides other than the hypotenuse.

For a right-angled triangle, then, if any two sides and an angle (apart from the right angle) are known, the length of the third side can be calculated. Similarly the angles can be calculated if the sides are known.

Appendix B:
Static and dynamic arrays

A static array is one that is prepared in advance before a program runs. For example, using DIM A%(100) will dimension an array of integers that consists of 101 integers (because A%(0) is the first member). Since an integer requires two bytes for storage, this statement will cause 202 bytes to be reserved before the program runs. This memory cannot be re-allocated to any other static array. If too much memory is assigned to an array, you will be informed by an error message before the program runs, which is before you start filling the array with data.

A dynamic array is one that is assigned while the program is running, using temporary memory. A dynamic array can be redimensioned, because this does not involve changing anything that has been fixed in advance, unlike the static array. The REDIM statement therefore always creates a dynamic array, and only a dynamic array can be redimensioned using REDIM.

A static array is created when a statement such as DIM A%(100) is used, specifying the size of the array by using a number (or more than one number for a multi-dimensional array). When a statement such as DIM A%(N%) is used, with a variable carrying the maximum size, the array is dynamic.

The type of arrays created by DIM can also be determined by using the meta-commands $STATIC and $DYNAMIC, each following a REM. Using either of these metacommands ensures that all arrays dimensioned following a metacommand will be of the defined type.

Appendix C: Segmented addressing in the PC machines

The 8-bit microprocessors that were used in the 1970s were able to address 65536 (64K) of different address locations, using 16 lines on which binary signals could be placed (since 2^{16} is 65536, FFFF in hexadecimal). When the 8088 and 8086 microprocessors were developed for the original IBM PC machine, it seemed logical to allow the methods that had been developed for the older machines also to be applied to the new ones.

The scheme that was adopted is called segmentation, and it allows for numbers higher than 65536 (FFFF) to be used by combining two numbers, each of which can take a maximum value of 65536 (FFFF). One of these numbers, each of 16-bits, is the segment number, the other is the offset address number, and the offset address number corresponds exactly with the address number that would have been used in the older 8-bit machines. This allowed for easy conversion of older software to the PC machine.

With the numbers written in hexadecimal, the final address number is obtained by shifting the segment number one place left and adding it to the offset number. For example, if the segment number is 2000 (hex) and the offset number is 0100 (hex), the final address is obtained by using:

$$\begin{array}{r} 2000 \\ \underline{0100} \\ 20100 \end{array}$$

which could be sent out on the 20 address lines of the 8086 and 8088 microprocessors.

The modern 80386DX and 80486 microprocessors use up to 32 address lines (the 80386SX machines use only 24) and keep numbers stored in 32 bit units, so that they can addressing memory directly with no need for segmented addressing. They can, however, be switched to using segmented address, called *real mode,* so as to be able to run programs under MS-DOS.

Appendix D: Environmental variables

Environmental variables are used to control the way that some aspects of MS-DOS work, and are also used along with some programs and with batch files. They provide a way of establishing conditions in advance by making an assignment to an environmental variable. For example, if the AUTOEXEC.BAT file for your computer contains the line:

PATH C:\; C:\MSDOS; C:\QBASIC

this establishes an environmental variable called PATH which MS-DOS uses to determine what directories to search for program files. The default is the directory that is currently in use, and if the required program is not in that directory the directories specified in PATH will be used. MS-DOS uses also the environmental variable (COMSPEC to find the command file), PROMPT (to control the type of screen prompt) and DIRCMD (to control the format of directory displays).

Several programs also make use of environmental variables to allow setting up to be done by external commands, usually in a batch file that runs the program. These will use the MS-DOS command SET in the format:

SET name = value

to set the variables for use in the program. You might, for example, want to set screen resolution, colour palette, mouse sensitivity and so on in this way. You can use only the environmental variables that your program can accept.

Appendix E:
Error number list

These are the QBASIC run-time errors which are delivered when a program stops due to a fault. The number is the error code that is contained in the variable ERR used in error-trapping routines.

No.	Error	No.	Error
1	NEXT without FOR	37	Argument-count mismatch
2	Syntax error	38	Array not defined
3	RETURN without GOSUB	40	Variable required
4	Out of DATA	50	FIELD overflow
5	Illegal function call	51	Internal error
6	Overflow	52	Bad file name or number
7	Out of memory	53	File not found
8	Label not defined	54	Bad file mode
9	Subscript out of range	55	File already open
10	Duplicate definition	56	FIELD statement active
11	Division by zero	57	Device I/O error
12	Illegal in direct mode	58	File already exists
13	Type mismatch	59	Bad record length
14	Out of string space	61	Disk full
16	String formula too complex	62	Input past end of file
17	Cannot continue	63	Bad record number
18	Function not defined	64	Bad file name
19	No RESUME	67	Too many files
20	RESUME without error	68	Device unavailable
24	Device timeout	69	Communication-buffer overflow
25	Device fault	70	Permission denied
26	FOR without NEXT	71	Disk not ready
27	Out of paper	72	Disk-media error
29	WHILE without WEND	73	Feature unavailable
30	WEND without WHILE	74	Rename across disks
33	Duplicate label	75	Path/File access error
35	Subprogram not defined	76	Path not found

Appendix F:
Screen modes

The following table summarises the screen mode numbers and their effects. Note that the assignment of colours using a noted number of attributes does not imply that all the colours can be on screen simultaneously. It is more usual to be able to use a range or palette of colours selected by attributes.

SCREEN 0: Text mode only

Use with: MDA, CGA, Hercules, Olivetti, EGA, VGA, or MCGA cards.

Text formats: 40 x 25, 40 x 43, 40 x 50, 80 x 25, 80 x 43, or 80 x 50

The standard character box is 8 x 8 , with 8 x 14, 9 x 14, or 9 x 16 available when EGA or VGA cards are used.

CGA and EGA allow 16 colours to be assigned using 16 attribute bits.

EGA and VGA allow 64 colours to be assigned using 16 attribute bits.

The number of video pages that can be used depends on the text resolution and the video adapter. The range of values for video pages is:
eight pages identified as 0-7
four pages identified as 0-3
two pages identified as 0-1
one page identified as 0

SCREEN 1: Text and graphics modes

Use with: CGA, EGA, VGA, or MCGA cards.

Text formats: 40 x 25
The standard character box is 8 x 8

Graphics formats: 320 x 200

CGA allows 16 background colours and one of two sets of three foreground colours to be assigned using a COLOR statement.

EGA and VGA allow 16 colours to be assigned using four attribute bits.

The range of values for video pages is:
one page identified as 0

SCREEN 2: Text and graphics modes

Use with: CGA, EGA, VGA, or MCGA cards.

Text formats: 80 x 25.
The standard character box is 8 x 8.

Graphics formats: 640 x 200.

EGA and VGA allow 16 colours to be assigned using two attribute bits.

The range of values for video pages is:
one page identified as 0

SCREEN 3: Text and graphics modes

Use with: Hercules, AT & T and Olivetti cards.

Text formats: 80 x 25.
The standard character box is 9 x 14.

Graphics formats: 720 x 348.

Monochrome only

The range of values for video pages is:
two pages identified as 0 - 1
one page (0) if a second video board is also present

NOTES: The PALETTE statement cannot be used along with SCREEN 3.
The driver MSHERC.COM must be used before starting QBASIC.

SCREEN 4: Text and graphics modes

Use with: Olivetti Personal Computer models M24, M240, M28, M280, M380, M380/C, and M380/T and AT&T Personal Computers 6300 series.

Text formats: 80 x 25.
The standard character box is 8 x 16.

Graphics formats: 640 x 400.

Background colour is always black. Foreground colour can be picked from a range of 16 colours using the COLOR statement.

The range of values for video pages is:
one page identified as 0

NOTES: The PALETTE statement cannot be used along with SCREEN 3

SCREEN 7: Text and graphics modes

Use with: EGA or VGA adapters.

Text formats: 40 x 25.
The standard character box is 8 x 8.

Graphics formats: 320 x 200.

A range of 16 colours can be assigned using 16 attributes.

The range of values for video pages is:
eight pages identified as 0 - 7 unless the video card contains only 64K of RAM, in which case only two pages (0 - 1) can be used.

SCREEN 8: Text and graphics modes

Use with: EGA or VGA adapters. Text formats: 80 x 25.

The standard character box is 8 x 8.
Graphics formats: 640 x 200.

A range of 16 colours can be assigned using 16 attributes.

The range of values for video pages is:
four pages identified as 0 - 3 unless the video card contains only 64K of RAM, in which case only one page (0) can be used.

SCREEN 9: Text and graphics modes

Use with: EGA or VGA adapters.

Text formats: 80 x 25 and 80 x 43.
The standard character box is 8 x 14 for 80 x 25, or 8 x 8 for 80 x 43.

Graphics formats: 640 x 350.

A range of 16 colours can be assigned using four attributes (64K memory) or 64 colours assigned to 16 attributes (using more than 64K memory).

The range of values for video pages is:
two pages identified as 0 - 1 unless the video card contains only 64K of RAM, in which case only one page (0) can be used.

SCREEN 10: Text and graphics modes

Use with: EGA or VGA adapters and monochrome monitor.

Text formats: 80 x 25 and 80 x 43.
The standard character box is 8 x 14 for 80 x 25, or 8 x 8 for 80 x 43.

Graphics formats: 640 x 350, monochrome.

A range of nine shadings can be assigned using four attributes.

The range of values for video pages is:
two pages identified as 0 - 1, with 256K of RAM used on the video card.

SCREEN 11: Text and graphics modes

Use with: VGA or MCGA adapters.

Text formats: 80 x 30 and 80 x 60.
The standard character box is 8 x 16 for 80 x 30, or 8 x 8 for 80 x 60.

Graphics formats: 640 x 480.

A range of 26624 colours can be assigned using two attributes.

The range of values for video pages is:
one page identified as 0.

SCREEN 12: Text and graphics modes

Use with: VGA adapter only.

Text formats: 80 x 30 and 80 x 60.
The standard character box is 8 x 16 for 80 x 30, or 8 x 8 for 80 x 60.

Graphics formats: 640 x 480.

A range of 26624 colours can be assigned using 16 attributes.

The range of values for video pages is:
one page identified as 0.

SCREEN 13: Text and graphics modes

Use with: VGA or MCGA adapters.

Text formats: 40 x 25.
The standard character box is 8 x 8. Graphics formats: 320 x 200.

A range of 26624 colours can be assigned using 256 attributes.

The range of values for video pages is:
one page identified as 0 .

Appendix G: QBASIC variable names and character set

Variable names used within QBASIC can consist of up to 40 characters and must begin with a letter. The valid characters are the letters A to Z, the numerals 0 to 9, and the full-stop (.). These names can be used for all internal purposes, but not for filenames which must conform to the MS-DOS limits of eight characters in the main part of the name with an options extension of up to three characters separated by a full-stop.

The QBASIC character set includes all of the alphabetic characters in upper-case (A to Z) and in lower-case (a to z), the numeric characters (0 to 9), including A to F or a to f for hexadecimal numbers, and the following list of characters which have special meanings in QBASIC:

!	Single-precision number.
%	Integer number.
#	Double-precision number.
&	Long-integer number.
$	String.

All of the above can be used to mark a variable name as being of a particular type. The alternative is to use a DIM statement for each variable name, declaring the type, and omitting any type suffix.

*	Multiplication.
-	Subtraction.
+	Addition.
/	Division (forward slash).
=	Relational operator or assignment symbol.
>	Greater than.
<	Less than.
.	Decimal point.
\	Integer division (backslash).
^	Exponentiation symbol.
'	Comment line (single quote).
;	Controls PRINT and INPUT statement output.
,	Controls PRINT and INPUT statement output.
:	Separates multiple statements on a single line.
?	INPUT statement prompt or PRINT abbreviation.
_	Line continuation underscore reserved for compatibility with other versions of BASIC but not supported by QBASIC.

Table G1. QBASIC mathematical operators